More praise for Zero to 80:

"The Impact team allows us to journey with them as they listen, l   nd lead a movement. Their stories invite us to rediscover the   and a passion to pursue a God-inspired dream. The   gies shared as a part of this remarkable jour   and replicable for healthy church star

*   .s,*

*   ~ Coach*

"No smoke and mirrors here — just hones   transparent people of God impacting their world in transform   .e ways. Every church planting team would be well served by reading and reflecting on this practical book together."

~Rev. Gary A. Shockley, Executive Director of Path 1,
New Church Starts at GBOD
and author of The Meandering Way

"Olu is a living, breathing embodiment of an effective, relevant, dynamic church pastor and shares in this book many of his beliefs, habits and practices. You will be blessed, if as you read, you catch hold of the BOLD SPIRIT that lives inside Olu; and then search for IT within yourself."

~Lawrence Young, District Superintendent in the Texas Annual
Conference of The United Methodist Church

"Zero to 80 is an indispensable guide for potential church planters and their supporters. This resource provides tools, ideas, stories and encouragement to help church leaders avoid being blindsided by subtle obstacles to starting and strengthening churches. I recommend Zero to 80 without reservation."

~Fred A. Allen, National Director of Strengthening
the Black Church for the 21st Century,
The United Methodist Church

"What a wonderful celebration of Impact's faith journey during its first two years. The congregation has shown personal strength, integrity and commitment during these exciting and challenging times. Zero to 80 is an inspiring read of an extraordinary journey!"

~Ingrid Saunders Jones, Senior Vice President,
The Coca-Cola Company

Eph 3:20 Trust God for your "r"

11/10/16

ZERO to 80

INNOVATIVE IDEAS FOR PLANTING AND ACCELERATING CHURCH GROWTH

OLU BROWN

AND THE IMPACT LEAD TEAM WITH CHRISTINE SHINN LATONA

!MPACT PRESS

Left to Right: Olu Brown, Anja Williams, Alan Jones, Maxine Fears, Dawn Wright, Sakon Kieh, Anika Jones and Edwin Turnipseed. (Alicia Ingram: Not pictured)

*The ideas in this book come from the practical wisdom
of the people named above who were on staff or in key volunteer
positions at the time of content generation. This content was
originally delivered via podcasts and then made into an audio CD
titled, Zero to 80: Starting a Church on the Run that Works.*

*To purchase the CDs or more copies of this book.
please visit us at www.0to80.org.
Volume discounts are available.*

ACKNOWLEDGEMENTS

Impact wishes to thank all those who helped make the vision a reality. Specifically, we thank God, our families, Impact attendees, The North Georgia Annual Conference of The United Methodist denomination and all of the dreamers who seek to push closer to the edge of opportunity. A special thanks to Christie Latona for partnering with us to make the dream of the book become a reality. Without her support and skill, the project would have remained a vision.

We dedicate this book to
our fellow Impactors.

Table of Contents

Small Groups — Drive to Reach Our God-Given Potential

Hospitality — Drive to Radical Customer Service

Worship — Drive to Worship Creatively

Logistics — Drive to Stay On Task, On Point and On Time

Staffing — Drive Toward a Staff-Led, Right Fit Model

Scheduled Maintenance — Drive Toward Effectiveness for the Long Haul

**Do you believe you hold the key
that can transform the world?**

Grab Your Keys

Welcome to a behind-the-scenes glimpse into the wonderful journey of a place called Impact Church. You are probably reading this book because you are thinking about, are responsible for, or are in the midst of planting a new congregation or growing an existing church. That means you don't have any time to waste, and we don't intend to waste your time with theories or hypotheses.

Impact launched worship in January 2007 with an advisory team of 25, attendance of 500 and six months' worth of planning that God blessed exceedingly. We write this to provide real-time ideas, stories and hope for our fellow church planting pioneers (or potential planters) who are pressing the gas pedal hard for God. At the beginning of 2008, we saw more than 1,000 in worship and raised more than one million dollars in donations at the close of the same year. This was a wonderful time in our short life span; a wonderful time of celebration.

As we reach new levels, Edwin Turnipseed (Support Pastor), reminds us of the importance of celebrating and reflecting with our team. Celebration, appreciation and reflection have been vital to our success. We intentionally celebrate each major milestone in a big way. We launched our children's ministry at the beginning of 2009 and celebrated by reminding the congregation of the sacred value of all of God's children and the responsibility of nurturing them in the way of Christ. We constituted Impact at the end of our 2009 with 413 charter members. We acknowledged all of the sweat, tears and prayers that helped launch the dream called Impact with a ceremony and celebration. Currently we are looking for more space and a more permanent ministry facility that will propel us into the next level of community ministry. And we will celebrate that accomplishment when it happens. We continuously seek God for what's "Next."

Throughout this book, we have shared the thoughts and real-time practices of some of the most dynamic leaders in new church planting — the Impact team, telling it from the heart. We hope the words written in these pages will challenge you and affirm what God has already told you to do.

The ideas in this book came from the Impact vision and individuals on the advisory team. We have tried to give credit where credit is due by noting the main contributor(s).

Each idea includes an invitation to "Make an Impact!" This is your chance to experiment with the idea in your context. While it may feel safer to just read the ideas and contemplate them, I would encourage you to take some risks and DO something with the ideas.

You cannot go from 0 to 80 without getting into the vehicle, putting on your seatbelt, starting the engine, putting it in gear, taking your foot off the brake and pressing the gas to the floor. You shouldn't go from 0 to 80 without clarity about the road ahead. One or more of these ideas just may provide the clarity you need to go from 0 to 80 in your context.

Here's to your journey,
Olu

DNA

DRIVE TOWARD GOD'S VISION AND DESIGN

mpact Idea

1

Name the Roads that Brought You Here

Olu

I have seen or experienced excellent ministry for most of my life. I was born in the small town of Lufkin, Texas, but had an ecumenical religious experience. Despite my parents' separation, I was blessed with a wonderful childhood. Nine months out of the year, my older siblings and I lived with my mother and attended two Baptist churches in our hometown. During the summer, we spent time with my father in Newark, New Jersey, where he served a local congregation as an ordained Presbyterian pastor.

When I was 13 years old, Lawrence Young came to Lufkin, Texas (my hometown) to plant a new church named Abundant Life United Methodist Church. Our family began to worship there. Abundant Life wasn't big on the orthodoxy, practice or doctrine of the church. Pastor Young was really big on building relationships. We connected to church in a whole new way. He became my mentor and still guides me to this day even though he's serving as a District Superintendent in the Texas Annual Conference of The United Methodist Church.

During my time at Abundant Life, I accepted my call to ministry and preached my first sermon as a senior in High School. When I went to Jarvis Christian College — founded by the Disciples of Christ — I experienced a campus church that captured my attention and exposed me to a different approach to ministry. When I completed college, I enrolled in The Interdenominational Theological Center in Atlanta, Georgia as a full-time graduate student. While there, I served as a part-time youth pastor at Cascade United Methodist Church. Upon graduation, I was fortunate enough to become a full-time Associate Pastor at Cascade.

Throughout my journey, I witnessed and experienced high capacity ministry firsthand and learned a great deal from observing the excellent leadership of Senior Pastor, Walter L. Kimbrough. Cascade had the ability to dream and cast vision toward the future while simultaneously executing plans for achieving those dreams.

I was impressed and frightened at the same time. I was blown away by the idea that God could use me in such a big way to do ministry.

 **MAKE AN IMPACT!**

Look back on your life and identify the roads and paths that have brought you to the place you currently feel called to go. What gifts, skills, ideas, lessons and memories will you carry forward?

Understand that Restlessness is a Vision Catalyst

Olu

A restless prophet in the Old Testament received a word of reassurance from God, "Write the vision; make it plain on tablets, so that a runner may read it." *Habbakkuk 2:2 (NRSV).* During one of the most difficult and troubling times in Habbakkuk's ministry, God spoke. I believe big vision grows out of our periods of restlessness and anxiety.

After about a year into my tenure as Associate Pastor at Cascade, I became undeniably restless. That feeling forced me to do a lot of self-examination. It forced me to review my call and purpose.

This restlessness worried me because Cascade was and is a great church. It hadn't changed — I had. Slowly it dawned on me that God was using all of the wonderful experiences and opportunities I had had at Cascade to prepare me for "next." I started wondering more and more about God's plan for my life and what God was calling me to do.

My restlessness was a vision catalyst for me. I became preoccupied with how to honor the creativity and spontaneity of our God by imagining and doing ministry in unpredictable and surprising ways. I became driven to find a way to meet the needs of the church and community without stifling the creativity within me and others — to free up staff and volunteers to go out into the world for Christ. According to John Maxwell, "Creativity is being able to see what everybody else has seen, what nobody else has thought, so that you can do what nobody else has done."[1]

I envisioned a place where people of all backgrounds could come and hear the Good News and somehow, through God's grace, develop into new creations. Though this idea was a tall order, I knew somehow it was possible.

Eventually, I realized that God was calling me to start a new church.

MAKE AN IMPACT!

Are there things in your present circumstance that make you feel restless? Make a list of those things in your community, your ministry, your relationships, and your encounters with others that make you angry, unsettled, exasperated and/or tempted to get up on your soapbox. What are you searching for?

See if you can fill three pages. Once you have emptied yourself, pray for God's wisdom in connecting the dots. Listen to God to discern where He is leading you.

Eclipse Fear with Faith

Olu

While I was simultaneously experiencing high capacity ministry and greater restlessness, God placed the idea of planting a new church on my heart. God revealed a new model of church within The United Methodist Church — something with a different form, larger scope, and more creative expression.

Me? Launch a whole new kind of church? I have never been so afraid. I was afraid of the responsibility and opportunity ahead. I was afraid that the vision was too big.

Over the years my mentor has drawn me back to *Ephesians 3:20 (NRSV)* "Now to him who by the power at work within us is able to accomplish abundantly far more than all we can ask or imagine." Imagine a God who has so much in store for us…a God who patiently waits on us to take the first step.

My first step was to tell my family and friends about God's vision. After much prayer and many conversations, I felt my faith growing stronger than my fear. Each affirmation I received expanded my faith until one day my fear was eclipsed by my faith.

After some of the fear went away, I realized God had been preparing me all my life. What an awesome revelation that was. And with that, I set the ball in motion. My first step was to tell my supervisor that I felt called to a new church start instead of being appointed to an existing church.

Little did I know! I did not have the capacity to even imagine what God had in store for me, my family, our advisory team and the folks who would one day represent the new church.

 **MAKE AN IMPACT!**

- What has God placed on your heart that you are afraid of?

- How has God been preparing you all your life for this vision?

- What do you need to do or to be reminded of in order for your faith to eclipse your fear?

- What is the next step you need to take to honor the vision God has given you?

Impact Idea 4
Dare to Vision Bigger at Every Step

Olu

I cannot express how important it is for you to VISION BIG. No matter how big your vision is — as long as God gave it to you in the first place — it does not make God afraid or cause God to become concerned.

Our vision started with the notion that I was to plant a new model within The United Methodist Church that evolved to include:

- A multi-cultural gathering of people who are committed to sharing the love of Christ with the world.
- "Doing Church Differently" so we reach people who aren't currently affiliated or attending church, and doing it in a way that makes people comfortable, surprised and excited.
- Core values of service, prayer, honesty, community, compassion and economic development.
- Giving back 10% of receipts to the community.
- Designing less bureaucratic or more flexible operational structures and systems.
- Relationships first, membership second.

Sometimes your vision can be so big, it frightens you and those around you. This is an ongoing process. As we were preparing to launch our first worship experience, I thought about donating a car or van during our first experience. I was visioning big. So big, I was afraid to tell some close friends about the crazy idea. Although ultimately we decided against the car/van donation, we considered it seriously even though it was really out of the norm.

Sometimes you have to exercise your faith to grow. You won't always hit the mark but I promise you that you won't be far from the target.

Throughout the crazy and unpredictable stuff that happened on our first day of worship, and all of the spectacular sacrifices that made it all possible, I was grateful to God for allowing us to vision big. We had dared to vision big and God blessed big.

As our team reflects on those first Sunday worship experiences, we cannot help but see God's grace. God not only came through for us, but God also richly blessed us. Looking back, I truly believe God blessed according to the vision.

If you think your vision is possible, it's not big enough. If you think you can't accomplish your vision, well, it's just about the right size. Our goal is to push you to the next level. I dare you to add 10 or 12 more ideas to your current vision.

When God gives us a big vision, we are instructed to write the vision on the wall. Remember Habbakkuk 2:2? Don't be afraid to publicize your vision when the right people are around and the right opportunity presents itself. Dare to dream impossible dreams!

MAKE AN IMPACT!

What big visions have been calling you? What big ideas would demonstrate your church's mission, purpose and core beliefs? It is time to dream limitless dreams. As you dream, write it down, type it, text it, Tweet it, Facebook it, scream it, pray it, cry it, laugh it. Whatever you do, do not hold it in. Trust God to make your vision come true. Dare to dream impossible dreams

Capture the Vision with Words — but Wait for the Right Ones to Find You.

Naming a new church is a discernment process that should not be rushed.

I wish I could tell you that the name for our new church start descended out of the sky, landed on the top of a mountain that I just happened to see as I was driving by and immediately I said, "That is it." Actually it found me another way. I was driving and listening to a song on the radio. Suddenly the artist mentioned the word "impact." Instantly, I knew "Impact" would be the name of the new church. I ran with it and I thank God for giving it to me.

As I sit in meetings or public gatherings, I laugh at how many times people say the word "impact." What is amazing is that in every arena and culture of life people use the word "impact," and I love it. Every time I hear "impact" it is as if God is confirming the name God gave to our church.

Later the phrase "Doing Church Differently" came about and it just stuck. As our team planned the launch, we always said we are "Doing Church Differently." It was funny when someone asked, "What does Doing Church Differently mean?" Our faces went blank. It's like explaining what the phrase "Just Do It" means.

Vision

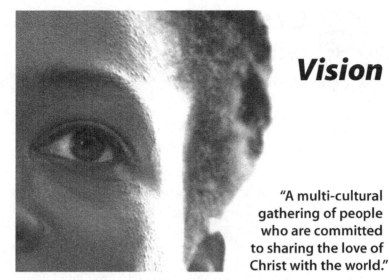

"A multi-cultural gathering of people who are committed to sharing the love of Christ with the world."

Core Values

Service

Prayer

Honesty

Community

Compassion

Economic Development

Get Comfortable with Who You Are

Olu and Edwin

The vision is going to come out of who you are both individually and collectively. It's going to come out of your experience. It's going to come out of your daily likes and dislikes. One of the most important things about building vision is just knowing and sharing who you are. It is vital to say with joy and acceptance, "Hey, this is how I came to know Christ; this is what I do and how I am as a result."

Beyond knowing who you are, you have to be comfortable in that knowledge. You have to take the good and the bad and say, "OK, here are the things that I like; here are the things that I dislike," and own it. Owning who you are makes vision possible.

God is still moving. God is still present. And God is still surrounding us with love. While doing church differently takes on various forms, the foundation is God's presence; knowing who you are and what God is calling you to do.

Generally, church planters and leaders have different motivations, different personalities, different gifts and different experiences. Leaders even have different pressures. Some of those pressures will come from a particular context, others from a particular denomination. The denomination is going to have a certain church planting push and/or philosophy. Individuals who are not affiliated with a denomination, may experience tension from financial or other types of supporters who push in certain directions they want to see the project go. Responding to these pressures needs to be balanced so that the leader continues to lead out of who they are, not out of who someone wants them to be.

Don't apologize for being who you are. What attracts people to you is the fact that you are authentic and you enthusiastically and consistently communicate that. People are attracted to vision and visionaries. The reason people will be attracted to your new church is because of your authentic, consistent vision and your transparency. Your steps and actions exude the presence of God. When you get comfortable with who you are and where God is leading, everything about you will show you are a visionary leader.

MAKE AN IMPACT!

Describe your comfort level with being who you are. Where and with whom are you freely sharing? Where and with whom are you holding back?

Can't Sit Still

I (Edwin) used to struggle with my restlessness because I used to think something was wrong with me. I can't be still; I can't sit down. Now I know it is just me being me. I am a person who is always thinking, wanting to get better, and to become a better person.

Olu and I get bored relatively easily. If there is no teaching component or learning component to whatever we are looking at being a part of — we simply aren't interested. Because of this, we continually push ourselves, our team leaders, and our teams to learn, grow and do new things. This shows up in all we do.

Do Church Differently

Olu and Edwin

Doing church differently comes from your God-given vision, personality, experiences, preferences and drive. Doing church differently, therefore, should look different in each context and under different leaders.

For us, doing church differently denotes creating and building relationships so that people feel comfortable, safe, and that they are learning new things in a different context. Doing church differently is combining all of those elements so that people enjoy themselves; that they have fun when they talk about what it means to be in a relationship with Jesus Christ, and that they can have fun when they walk into a worship experience.

For us, doing church differently is about constant innovation and surprise. We understand that people might get bored after a year or two in typical church settings — settings that are predictable physically, programmatically and in other dimensions. A part of doing church differently is simply reaching people in a very creative, unique, fun and relevant space. We have a paradigm of church where things are done in a particular way and context: "This is how it's always done." For us, doing it differently doesn't say that we're going to throw out the old, but it simply says, "We are going to try a creative, fun, relevant model that is delightfully different!"

MAKE AN IMPACT!

1. Draw a box.
2. Write words inside the box that represent doing "typical" church that don't fit with who you are and who you seek to reach.
3. Put things outside the box that represent what doing church differently may look like, given who you are and who you seek to reach.
4. Circle the things you consistently communicate in word and in your actions. The circled words can show you what doing church differently may look like based on who you are and the context in which you minister.

Throw Limitations Out the Window

Olu

Some people ask me, "What is the secret to church growth?" I say there is no special secret other than trusting God and throwing the limitations out of the window. I could fill these pages with spoken and unspoken limitations. Some limitations are superficial or circumstantial. For example:

- My family won't support a new church.
- My denomination won't approve a new church.
- My key contributors just walked away.
- The people in this town just aren't interested in God.
- There isn't any land for a church.

Others are more personal and can seem even more insurmountable:

- I can't raise enough money.
- I am not a good enough administrator.
- I am not prepared enough, good enough, smart enough, tall enough, (etc.) to start a new church.

Although each of these limitations may be real to you and to your context, they are not challenging to God. Trust God more than you have ever trusted God in your life.

If you are feeling more focused on the limitations than on God's possibilities, I strongly suggest you seek out people who truly inspire you and discover the places that cause you to dream.

In the next few months, bend your calendar time and focus toward those people and places. Go to the dreamers in your

Limitations Out the Window... Faith Forward

midst and spend as much time with them as possible. Spend the majority of your precious moments with people who are positive thinkers — people who believe in the promises of God for greater things. This is a time to seek out those who are constantly striving towards the next level of blessing, faith, hope and development.

MAKE AN IMPACT!

- Who inspires you?

- What places or environments inspire you?

- Which people in your life give you more energy instead of more worry?

- Who in your circle of family, friends and acquaintances has demonstrated that they believe with God nothing is impossible?

Look at your answers to the above questions and spend more time in the next several months with those people and in those environments that will help you stay focused.

Demonstrate Vision in Relevant Ways

Impact Idea 8

Olu and Edwin

Perhaps one of the greatest vision moments was "Impact Giving Back." Early on, we decided that it would be important for Impact to give back ten percent of our receipts to the community and model what we were asking others to do.

We both feel that Impact Giving Back has probably contributed to most of our "success" — whatever you call success in church planting. The concept was developed even before we had our first worship service. It was part of our DNA.

Impact Giving Back started as a very basic way of saying we want to make sure that no matter what happens in the community, we want to be a part of it — including financially. We also seek to give more than we take in our community. Impact seeks to be relevant to the community that it is serving.

In one of my previous jobs, I witnessed a unique approach to strong partnership building. This particular partner simply showed up occasionally to find out what we needed. He would do this first before making any offers, recommendations, solutions or suggestions as to how his organization could help ours. That particular concept was one of the contributing factors that helped spark the idea of Impact Giving Back.

In our first quarter of worship (Q1 2007), we gave a significant financial donation to the school and to the administrator, each staff person, and teacher where we worshipped. We were in awe of the immediate impact those gifts had on our relationship with the school and the testimonies that resulted from them.

Brown Middle School is located in the heart of the West End community of Atlanta. We talked about being partners with key stakeholders; and so we asked, "Why not here?" We took $8,000 and got a directory of all the staff, the teachers, the principals, the para-professionals, the custodians and the cafeteria workers. We even took down names of folks involved in staffing specific projects. The final list included 80 people. We decided to give $1,000 to the school and divide the remaining $7,000 among the list of 80 people as gift cards.

We made this contribution at a time when monetary assistance was least expected — not at the beginning of the school year or around the holidays. It was right about the time when they were getting ready to do their standardized graduation tests. At that time teacher morale can be down and stress high. We walked into the school building and presented the principal with the $1,000 check — not in any formal ceremony, we just walked in and presented the check. She was in a meeting and came out to accept it. She was excited about it, but obviously it wasn't the first time they'd been given money by a church. The principal was in a rush to get back to the meeting, so we asked the receptionist to give a bag to her. In the bag were the 80 gift cards with $87 loaded on each card.

We got an email from the principal a couple of days later. She was overwhelmingly grateful and said, "We've never been able to give our staff or faculty anything like this before. How are we supposed to give it?" We reaffirmed the purpose of our donation: she got to decide how to distribute the gift cards as long as she made sure that everybody received one.

This is an example of how we intentionally focused on giving, not on receiving credit for the gift. We did not need applause. We did not need attention or a formal ceremony that was focused on our gifts.

We wanted all the staff and support folks to understand our purpose. We just wanted to tangibly convey, "Impact appreciates you and supports your efforts to educate the students!"

This is in line with our goal to attempt to give back at least 10% of what we were blessed with. We feel like we have been blessed because we have been able and willing to bless so many people.

We remember sharing the good news with the Impact congregation. We felt like we were on top of the world because we were showing people how to vision big and to give big. We were not holding anything back for the Kingdom. We were out of the box going 400 mph with no brakes or emergency off switch.

MAKE AN IMPACT!

What is your personal and organizational level of generosity? How do people know? Pray that God will lead you to be more generous and for ways you may live that new level in a big way — personally and organizationally.

Repel Self-Centered Growth

Olu

The initial core vision and product grows out of the initial or root leadership. This is why it is important for the core group to have an understanding of where the plan is headed and to be as diverse as possible. Vision alignment keeps you focused. Diversity keeps you engaged in the culture.

I hand selected the lead team. I intentionally chose people for their passion for the vision, their skill and ability in particular areas of need, and for the quality of our personal relationship. I found that you need to be friends or have the high potential to be friends with each person who is in that initial group, because planting is so intense and so "all in." Additionally, I sought to ensure that the leaders represented the community we were trying to attract.

I called them the advisory team; not the lead team, to avoid the pitfall of people living into a title of esteem too quickly.

During the initial launch phase, we took special care to build the Impact brand around the vision and not the "lead" pastor or other founding leaders. We clearly understood that during the church's pre-launch stage, most people would be attracted to the lead person or persons but we constantly fought against allowing this trend to extend into our launch phase. I often said one of my goals in the early days of the church plant was to decentralize me.

There are churches where the marketing, wealth and power flow around the senior or lead pastor only. That dynamic can happen in new church planting as well. In fact, some church consultants may push for the lead or franchise player to be the poster child for the organization, always out front. In some contexts this approach may work, but it needs to be assessed and questioned consistently to avoid difficulties down the road.

From day one, we intentionally designed teams and ministry approaches that invited people (other than me) to be empowered and have authority. We take seriously the priesthood of all believers.[2] We do not use my name and face on marketing material. The role of clergy is respected but not set apart architecturally, in dress or in any other way. We intentionally blur lines between clergy and laity to expand our leadership pool and level the playing field of commitment and involvement.

Neither the growth nor the health of Impact revolves around one person. Instead, a group of engaged leaders ensures that expansion occurs more rapidly and in more dynamic ways. Essentially expansion happens exponentially at Impact.

 **MAKE AN IMPACT!**

In your organization, are you the only green light? Are you the sole authority that can give people permission to launch new projects and ideas? If so, pray that God will lead you to delegate your authority and nurture other leaders for the sake of the legacy of the organization and innovation.

Advisory Teams and First Organization Chart

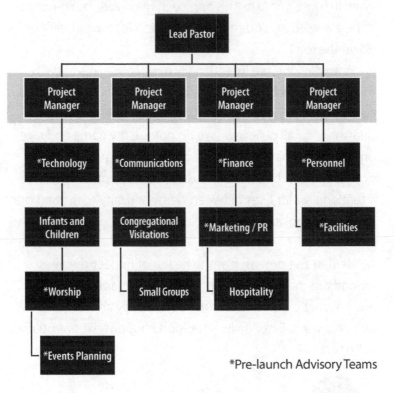

Lead Pastor

Project Manager | Project Manager | Project Manager | Project Manager

*Technology | *Communications | *Finance | *Personnel

Infants and Children | Congregational Visitations | *Marketing / PR | *Facilities

*Worship | Small Groups | Hospitality

*Events Planning

*Pre-launch Advisory Teams

Impact Idea 10

Become a High-Functioning Organization

Olu

Let me tell you why history was made on the day of our first worship experience in January 2007. History was made because we formed a group of individuals as our core team. Some of those individuals were from younger generations; some from older generations, but over a six-month planning period, we came together as a family--as a core team. And so, history was made internally because we took people with diverse backgrounds and because we knew that part of our ultimate vision was reaching un-churched or de-churched, or over-churched people. We knew we needed to connect with folks who weren't overly religious.

Our core team was made up of people with prior faith backgrounds and those with limited faith backgrounds. In the end, we developed a group of passionate people driven by the vision of the possibility of Impact Church.

As I consider the great movements throughout the world, I have noticed that many of them were started by small groups of people with big dreams. I hope you are inspired to know that you do not need vast numbers of people on your initial team. You only need a small group of the "right people" on your team.

In his masterwork, *Good to Great*, Jim Collins reminds us of the need to have the right high-functioning people on the team. He said, "The main point is to first get the right people on the bus (and the wrong people off the bus) before you figure out where to drive it."[3]

This idea is critical if you are planning to build a highly functional family of leaders who will help launch and lead the organization into the future. I know this sounds tough, but your group is only as good as the team that is organized to lead it. My hope is that you will take the time to critically and prayerfully select the right initial leaders who will help move the program forward. Also, if you discover you don't have the right people on board, I pray you will offer them clear directions to the exit door and make the right choices for the new organization.

MAKE AN IMPACT!

Who do you need on your team based on the current or future needs of the organization? What are your criteria for a team member? Who is on your team that needs to get off the team? When was the last time you prayed for the power of discernment to assist you in selecting the right person for the team?

Relationships

DRIVE TO ASK "HOW CAN WE HELP?"

Impact Idea 11

Shift from Taking to Helping

Edwin

We develop real-life relationships in the community where we worship and the community beyond simply by asking, "How can I help you?"

In many instances, churches are not fully valued by their communities. This can happen when some people believe that the church is a place that "takes." They "take" a weekly donation, "take" an hour or so for worship every Sunday and maybe even ask for donations of time, talent and treasure. At Impact, we work very hard to change this perception of the church. When we reach out to the community we ask questions like, "How can we assist you in accomplishing your vision?"

Many church planters don't launch in a traditional church setting, but in a school or other space that is used for a different purpose other days of the week. We encourage planters to do more than have church in the space on Sunday morning — we encourage planters to build relationships and partnerships.

Brown Middle School, the place where we worship on Sundays, has become a place of ministry and rich relationships. Through intentional relationship building, we are volunteering or have presence in Brown Middle School Monday through Friday.

Our relationship with the school began when I thought, "Wow, this is a great opportunity to minister." Deep inside, I believed we could make strides there and that they would see us as an ally. Of course, some members of the staff were skeptical at first.

I had a conversation with the principal because I wanted to know how we could help. Eventually, I connected with other members of the school such as the CIS area, which is Communities in Schools, and met the coordinator. I told her that we wanted to help.

She said she had never had a partner just walk up and say "Tell us where we can help." Most people would approach her with their plans or their ideas before getting to know them or their needs. Because we approached the school staff with a spirit of curiosity and generosity, they were more receptive to our dollars and more receptive to the fact that there might be people from Impact who were willing to mentor.

When you want to be a part of the contextual community you have to go in and ask, "How can we help?" If you want to build relationships, you cannot go into an existing organization, make demands and hold the organization hostage with your potential donations. This approach closes the doors to communication and progress. When it comes to building significant relationships, you can totally change the dynamic of how people perceive you and relate to your church in their community. Always remember the big question to ask is, "How can I help you?"

MAKE AN IMPACT!

This is simple. Identify three new significant relationships you want to form in your community. When you set up the meeting, let them know that you want to learn about how you can contribute to their efforts.

Listen carefully and ask questions to ensure you understand them. Ultimately your partnership develops from your experience and the voices of those you are interviewing.

Invest in Key Stakeholders

Olu and Edwin

Take a look at your community. Who are the key stakeholders? Who are the people you need to invite to lunch or dinner? Who are the people on the streets that you need to be shaking hands with? Who are the folks sitting on the porch wondering if and when you will stop by and see them? Key stakeholders aren't going to come see you first — they're waiting for you to reach out to them.

Key stakeholders include business owners, local businesses, hospitals, social service agencies, schools, community centers, and residents. We visited almost all of our community stakeholders before we launched Impact Church and believe this helped us significantly. We spent time telling our story and we presented opportunities for our stakeholders to ask questions and share their concerns.

We went beyond casual conversations and actually started to invest in some of our stakeholders. One of our pre-worship experiences occurred at a local arts center located on the main thoroughfare. Subsequently, we have rented the space for other events. Leasing the space not only showed us giving more than taking (we didn't ask to use space for free), but it also got us deeper into the mission field.

We have had the pleasure of meeting people who have shared, "I remember you all, because you were over in XYZ venue." It is a visible sign that church doesn't happen only on Sunday mornings; that church can also be associated with something occurring within other contexts or communities.

We think it is especially important to sow seeds into the life of the venue you inhabit as meeting space. We let the principal at Brown Middle School know we did not want to be just tenants. We also wanted to be integrated into the life of the school. Creating this reality solidified our relationship with our stakeholders and created a positive impression: *these people aren't merely in our building on Sunday morning — they want to make a difference in the community.*

Once people see you trying to mingle and show support for their agenda, then you become their ally. They stop viewing you as an outside entity that is only using "their" place to attract people who don't care, aren't connected to, or aren't invested in the community.

A mentor of mine posed a powerful question to congregations that are seeking to define or determine their impact: "If you were no longer in that community, would they miss you?" *Would they miss you?* Now that's key! I think about that every time we're walking anywhere within our target community. Do people know we're here? If we weren't here, would they notice it?

MAKE AN IMPACT!

Brainstorm a list of your potential key stakeholders. Key stakeholders include business owners, local businesses, hospitals, social service agencies, schools, community centers, residents, etc.

With your long list in hand, make a plan to visit as many of those as possible.

The purpose of your visit is threefold: to let them know you exist, to demonstrate that you give more than you take (don't ASK them for anything), and to discover how you can help.

Let the venue where you are meeting know that you want to integrate into their life.

Give Back More Than You Take

Olu and Edwin

Our ultimate goal is to give back more than we take. Sadly, a lot of congregations are guilty of taking more than they give. At Impact Church we are intentional about giving strategically in our community — not giving so that our name can be in the newspaper — but giving because it is a part of our mission.

"Impact Giving Back" is how we describe our discipline of attempting to give back at least ten percent of our income. In some cases giving back may be a direct cash transaction. In other cases it may mean buying t-shirts for the football team or the basketball team. It may involve buying a hardware product that a local business or a local community center needs (e.g., computers or telephones). At the end of the day, we must make sure we are giving more than we're taking.

It was a difficult concept for some of our team leaders to grasp at first. It helped when they saw the congregation react to our implementation of that value. On a quarterly basis during our worship experience, we announce what we've given back so all can witness the integrity and value in our process.

For example, let's say we've collected $120,000.00 in a particular quarter. 10% of that is $12,000.00. We look through the statements for the quarter, and discover we have given away $9,000.00. So we meet with a group of leaders who help us decide how to give away the remaining $3,000.00. This creates so much excitement for the team that when they go to share our giving, authentic enthusiasm permeates the atmosphere. It gets the congregation excited. Ultimately, we try to model what we ask each individual to do when we ask them to tithe. One of our mentor coaches said, "If the church models stewardship, then worshippers will say, 'If tithing is what the church is doing, then I can do it also.'"

When you want to build a good relationship, give more than you take.

MAKE AN IMPACT!

Decide how much and what you're willing to give. If you are in a new church start, do this as soon as possible to build it into the DNA. If you are in an existing congregation, decide what you're willing to give before you launch that new ministry or that new site.

Bridge the Gaps
Olu and Edwin

It is vital that church planting teams go into new places or new communities without their blinders on. We miss significant relationship opportunities when we judge a book by its cover. The book can be a person, a group of people, or a community.

We happened to launch our new church in an urban community. There are a lot of things said about big city urban communities that are really untrue. Two of our favorite myths are:

1. Everybody in an urban community is poor; and
2. Everybody in an urban community lacks a higher level of education.

In our community, these two things are absolutely not true. If you are operating out of hearsay, myth, or common misperceptions, you can overlook people who have power and influence.

The Bible talks about entertaining angels unaware. My hope is that whatever your ministry context is — whether it's near a hospital or local business or local school or a major residential development — you would look at everyone as an angel, as someone of divine value and worth. You will never know the dynamics of the relationship that can take place, or what God has in store, if you fail to take the time to invest in somebody else.

Moreover, it is necessary to invest in somebody before you can help fill in or bridge the gaps. Looking at some of the relationships we have right now, we realize many were not relationships we had anticipated. Some were fostered out of a need from another relationship. Often we become a bridge that connects a community entity that has a need with an entity that has a surplus in that area of need. For example, through our relationship with a local school and a local donut shop in Atlanta, when the school needs an extra sweet something, we are able to ask the donut shop to meet that need. We can fill the gap because we have built a relationship with the proprietors.

Through the efforts of our new church, a local coffee shop is getting involved with our target school as well. Early on, we realized our unique position in the neighborhood. Impact became relevant and vital to the community by being a bridge builder among the key stakeholders.

MAKE AN IMPACT!

Listen deeply as those in your community describe their needs and seek to be a matchmaker between their needs and another entity's purpose.

Build Relationships Through Giving

Edwin

We like to use our Experience Giving process (that's what we call our offering) as a teaching tool for our values. We have done things within Experience Giving that blow people's minds. One Sunday we didn't even take up an offering. Instead, we instructed people to use what they would have given Impact to bless someone else. Folks were asked to write down the amount of money they were planning to give to Impact and also write the name of someone they knew who might need financial assistance. Then we encouraged them to give their offering to the person they listed.

This process was an awesome step in building relationships. People might be aware of an individual or organization in need of support, but haven't taken the time to build a relationship. We thought if we empowered our people to give seed money to individuals or organizations, the action would spark them to build relationships. By giving people a financial blessing, we can start a dialogue that begins to build relationship. Moreover, since the money comes from an unusual gesture initiated by the church, it gives people a chance to share a bit about Impact Church. They may say, "I was getting ready to donate money to my church, but we were asked to do something different this Sunday. Impact asked us to give the money to a person who needed the money — someone we have seen while traveling to or from church. I thought of you. Here, I need to bless you." Lots of dialogue and relationships were sparked that week!

The Impact person who provided the financial blessing is more visibly positioned to be the transformation agent. While some people get stuck on the financial aspect of this, it really goes back to building relationships. Money, in this example, is an outward and visible sign that: I noticed a need; I care and I want to invest in you.

Some of you could be shaking your heads about doing something as radical as this, thinking people in the congregation wouldn't go for it. This idea didn't come from Olu or me — it came from our lead finance person.

MAKE AN IMPACT!

Take some time at your next meeting with church leaders to review this idea. Then ask: *What is a simple thing we can do to empower all people who participate in our ministry to be transformation agents?*

Be Touchable

Edwin

Impact Idea 16

Believe it or not, some people who plant new faith communities struggle to produce fruit because they don't do a great job developing new relationships. Not that they couldn't be good at it, it's just not that high on their priority list.

Church planters can become absorbed in the administrative work and the mundane tasks that we have to do day to day. It is easy to lock ourselves into an office space or a location that is isolated from people, working on that next sermon or figuring out the next strategy. However, part of that next great sermon, part of that next great growth strategy comes from being in relationship with the community. We have to build significant relationships with people in the community. If people don't know about you, it's not their fault. It could be your fault.

I've gotten sermon ideas merely by seeing somebody walk into the room and watching them interact with somebody else. I always ask myself, "What if I had not been here? Would I have had that as a launching point for a sermon?"

And we have to go beyond observation. Engaging in dialogue with people in the community should cause them to feel, "This person is authentic — I can touch them. They will tell me what they think." The best way to engage is by being present in simple, basic ways. We don't always have to schedule individual appointments on the calendar. Often it is more important for us to show up in the places where people naturally gather; not in any formal way, but in open, transparent ways. While sitting in a community center or being in a local coffee shop, or even just walking up and down the street, we are perceived as people who are available to talk about anything and everything at any time.

We ought to be in the business of transforming lives. We can transform somebody's life only if they know us. If I can enter into a relationship with them, and from that relationship, they see my relationship with Jesus Christ, then guess what's going to happen? They're going to want that same relationship.

Before we can ultimately transform someone's life, the person has to trust and touch us first. Instead of starting at point A, sometimes we want to jump to Q, or T, or S, or whatever the letter is. At the same time, the other person is wondering, "What happened to just shaking my hand? What happened to having a cup of tea or coffee with me? What happened to coming to my school and eating lunch with me? What happened to coming to my game?" All are examples of starting at point A.

In the Impact worship context, attendees may not hear a verbal invitation to accept Jesus Christ every week. Although accepting Christ is important to us, we realize that building relationships is critical to our success in guiding someone into a new relationship with Jesus Christ. We are very intentional about developing significant relationships inside and outside of the worship experience. Being touchable is the key to making life change happen.

 **MAKE AN IMPACT!**

Take a week or two and track your time in the following categories:

- Administration

- Sermon and/or Teaching Preparation

- Building Significant Relationships with Individuals

- Building Significant Relationships with the Community

- Developing Strategies for Growth

Before you track your time, identify your first, second and third priority from the above categories. See if the actual time spent matches your priorities.

What percentage of your time is spent being present in the community? What percentage is spent building significant relationships inside and outside of the worship experience?

Decentralize Transformation

Olu and Edwin

Our personal relationships enable us to introduce Jesus Christ to others. The notion that only the paid staff or pastors or certain lay leaders can "lead people to Christ" is one of the barriers we have found in the church. This idea or thought process gets in the way of personal relationships that transform.

We have found it necessary to remind everyone that when they find themselves in situations where they can lead somebody to Christ, they should do it right then and there! Don't wait for a staff person or pastor. It is much more meaningful and natural for a fellow believer or a child of God to walk with them on that journey than to bring them to someone they do not know.

There is more to the transforming moment than just saying to them, "Okay, you're received." It's about being in relationship with that person. You know their story. They know your story. It is powerful to be in relationship with somebody and they say to you, "It's because of you that I know Jesus Christ. It's because of you that I know what Jesus really means."

We encourage our leaders to view themselves as ministers to those they have relationships with and to those with whom they will build relationships. As disciples of Jesus Christ, it should be a natural part of our relationships with others to become their minister. This approach is not only natural; but it is also necessary. One person can minister to only a few people effectively. We are seeing over 1,000 people each weekend at Impact and many more throughout the week. Despite our best efforts, we are unable to spend quality time with all the people connected to Impact. Therefore, we try to guide team leaders and people who are around us and model for them what they need to do to help others. Then, the leaders train and model for their teams and so forth. This system decentralizes the role of the pastors and enables us to be the hands of Christ more profoundly and in more places than we can imagine.

We know that Christ has no hands but ours. If we emulate servant leadership in our leading, then people will see our good works, enter into a relationship, and seek to become the hands of Christ as well.

MAKE AN IMPACT!

What type of leadership are you modeling? Is it easy to replicate? How are you encouraging people to take ownership and leadership for leading people to Christ?

Decentralized, Transformational Viability

Develop Individual and Community Economic Viability

Olu and Edwin

Economic development is one of our core values. It is an essential part of our church and we believe it should be emphasized by churches worldwide. We cannot fully address spiritual needs without also addressing the non-spiritual part of people's everyday lives.

We believe in taking a holistic approach to ministry. Reverend Kirbyjon Caldwell, pastor of Windsor Village United Methodist Church in Houston, Texas, said it best when he referred to "holistic salvation." This concept compels congregations to see each person as a whole being with spiritual, physical, mental, social, and economic needs.[4]

When people and communities are empowered to meet both financial and spiritual needs, the world will begin to change for the better. Developing communities and serving as a positive change agent are important parts of the core vision of Impact Church. Our work in the area of economic development has helped us gain credibility and access in ways we would not have been able to accomplish by typical church-based conversations alone.

Wouldn't it be great if economic development were the norm and not the exception? Where churches collectively decided that there was far more to Christ than beautiful hymns, softly whispered stories and a Christmas play? After the hymn, stories and play end, people return to their real worlds.

As the church of today, we have to decide to impact the real world by meeting people in it.

MAKE AN IMPACT!

How are you caring for the holistic needs — spiritual, physical, mental, social, and economic — of your people and your community? Is this central to your ministry or an afterthought?

Relationships First, Membership Later

Olu and Edwin

Each weekend, over 1,000 people worship at Impact; how-ever, none of them are regarded as members. Though mem-bership in our church culture matters from a commitment standpoint, in our present-day culture, "a sense of belonging" trumps or surpasses "a habit of joining."

When we first launched Impact, we decided that we would not focus on membership, but we would focus on relation-ships. We understood there was a cultural shift in the wind related to relationships and memberships. Because our main target was to reach the un-churched, we knew we could not hang out after church holding an outdated clipboard with a piece of cardstock clamped on asking people to join. Frankly, this would have been the worst approach we could have taken and would have resulted in anti-church growth. Instead, we were in our target community having conversations with peo-ple; we clearly understood people wanted relationship first.

You can imagine how surprised everyone was when we did not ask them to become a member of Impact during or after a worship experience or event. We focused on building significant relationships with the people first, because we real-ized their commitment would come later. I was in awe when I traveled to local venues and people who came to Impact would introduce me as their pastor. Even though technically they were not members of Impact, they had enough of a rela-tionship with Impact to consider me their pastor.

We have discovered that if you take significant time building relationships, then membership is an easy formality. When we did begin offering membership, we invited people to officially join Impact, we sought to continue to honor our brand of "doing church differently." Today we don't refer to people at Impact as "members," rather we call them "Impactors." An Impactor is someone committed to more than the denomination. It is someone committed to the way of Christ and making an impact in the world. As you think about membership — or rethink membership — hope you give much thought to building relationships first.

 **MAKE AN IMPACT!**

What is the difference between joining your church versus participating in your church? How are you demonstrating the principle of relationships first?

Marketing

DRIVE TO EXPAND AWARENESS, FOCUS, AND REACH

Impact Idea 20

View Marketing as Outreach with Vibe

Olu and Alicia

In the for-profit world, marketing is a clearly understood concept. Marketing is about doing what is necessary to sell something. These sales are vital to creating profits which are necessary to stay in business. Conversely, in the for-profit world, creating profits equates to fulfilling a mission. In a church setting, marketing is a type of ministry outreach. Looking at it in those terms, we have the best product out there.

Some of you may have issues with our saying the church has a "product." However, it doesn't cheapen the Gospel to talk about salvation and transformation using that metaphor. It is the best product out there and it is the responsibility of each disciple to get the world to understand it in a way that will help diverse groups of people connect with Jesus and the life He offers.

Our brand: "doing church differently," affects our marketing philosophy as well. Our goal is to market church differently to reach people creatively and uniquely in spaces where they typically don't see churches.

As we go about making Atlanta aware of our Impact Church brand, we are seeking to create multiple positive impressions, and to build a relationship between the "consumer" and Impact. A brand is not just the name or the look, but it is a particular feeling — it's the vibe associated with a particular organization. From a church perspective, it's about people knowing and feeling what you stand for through your vibe.

Marketing needs to create more than name recognition. It needs to create a vibe — an expectation of what they get anytime they see, hear, touch, smell, feel something from Impact.

To help people understand the vibe of "doing church differently" we're looking at things that haven't been done before by churches in our area; in having a presence at events where churches don't normally participate. For example, one of the things we're looking at is movie theatre marketing. We're thinking of putting an Impact invitation in the midst of all the movie previews — in a space where people don't expect to see a plug for a church.

Marketing at theatres is just one example of how we are seeking to reach people in places they go in their everyday lives. The way we show up in those places aligns with the culture more than with traditional images and notions of what church is. We don't have a traditional look and feel. We know we are on the right track when people tell us that Impact marketing doesn't look like a church.

In the Impact culture, if a marketing piece (e.g., flyer, billboard or worship graphic) looks like a church, it fails to convey our vibe. We realize — for the most part — Impact is trying to reach the folks who don't identify with this "churchy" look. We believe they need something innovative that relates directly to their context.

MAKE AN IMPACT!

What vibe are you creating with your marketing? What do you need to change in order to position your marketing to be a powerful outreach ministry?

Get Professional Marketing Help

Alicia, Olu, Edwin

The groups we seek to reach don't respond positively to images that evoke unprofessional, traditional, static church. Often churchy, homemade flyers are created because there is no professional design and/or no vision for marketing as outreach. While there is nothing inherently wrong with that, it may not create the impression you are seeking to create in order to reach the people you are seeking to reach. If you want a positive result, it's important that you invest in professional looking materials that capture attention. Professional designers know how to do just that.

Of course, we learned our lesson the hard way through a marketing piece that Olu and Edwin designed themselves. That experience convinced us that we had to find somebody who could translate the vision into something that would excite the culture we were seeking to reach. While we started with a simple 4 by 6 inch postcard, we had a long-range vision of using large 14 by 48 feet billboards. We wanted to market at that level; however, we lacked the skills to get us there. We started recruiting volunteer marketing people and allocating funds for design. Eventually we reached the point where we hired a staff-level marketing expert to oversee design, creativity and placement decisions.

At this juncture, we have a professional staff person dedicated to Communications and Marketing. She is empowered to make marketing happen. She selects the designers, decides how to spend the marketing budget, and coordinates the volunteer marketing team. Since she has taken leadership of this area, our materials have an edgy, professional, sleek look and feel that rivals any contemporary commercial you see out there. She knows that is the space and the attention we're competing for, and she ensures our ads are competitive creatively, thematically and culturally.

As you share ideas, you may choose not to reveal to new designers that the project is for a church, because that can trigger an impulse to throw a bible or a cross here and put a photo of the pastor there. Tell them, to be "edgy" not "churchy."

The notion and expense of professional design can be overwhelming. It makes good sense to start one project at a time, one step at a time, one bulletin, one flyer, one billboard at a time. For example, we utilized billboards as a part of our marketing strategy from the beginning, but we didn't start at the largest size. We started small and have worked our way up to 14 by 48. So while we had a dream of running these huge billboards, we couldn't start there. We had to start at another level, and we worked our way up to the billboard dream.

In some churches, the evangelism ministry became the default marketing team as well. In most cases, the evangelism team does not ask for the job and was not prepared to execute the marketing vision of the church. To create the first impression you desire and achieve the best result, hire a professional to do the job.

MAKE AN IMPACT!

What is your marketing dream? What is your most important marketing piece? Does it communicate your vibe? Are there any materials you need to retire because they don't communicate your vibe? How much does your organization invest in marketing?

Make Sure You Use Designers Who Get It

You can waste a lot of time, energy and money when interacting with a designer who doesn't get it. We had an experience with a designer in our logo process. We experienced some design challenges with getting a first logo that we even remotely liked. We said we were a church and we got back "churchy" stuff.

Even though we explained the vision of doing church differently two to three times, the designer had difficulty grasping the concept. Sometimes it is better if you're able to have someone who is an in-house professional do your designs, or stick with someone who has worked with your organization and understands your organization and its vision.

The best Pre-Game Experience in Atlanta!

Experience Schedule

SEPTEMBER
SM ◼ September 13th - 10 only
SM ◼ September 20th - 10 only
GA ◼ September 27th - 10 & 12

OCTOBER
TM ◼ October 4th - 10 & 12
SM ◼ October 11th - 10 & 12
TM ◼ October 18th - 10 & 12
SM ◼ October 25th - 10 & 12

NOVEMBER
SM ◼ November 1st - 10 & 12
SM ◼ November 8th - 10 only
GA ◼ November 15th - 10 & 12
SM ◼ November 22nd - 10 & 12
SM ◼ November 29th - 10 only

DECEMBER
SM ◼ December 6th - 10 only
SM ◼ December 13th - 10 only
SM ◼ December 20th - 10 & 12
◼ December 27th - No Services
Impact Day of Sabbath

JANUARY 2010
SM ◼ January 3rd - 10 & 12 noon

www.impactaed.org

◻ **FALCON'S AWAY GAME**
Services at 10:00 a.m. & 12:00 noon
Parking available in the RED LOT.

◻ **FALCON'S HOME GAME**
Services at 10:00 a.m. ONLY
Parking available in the YELLOW LOT.

✓ Falcon's game time will not affect worship schedule. Two Services and parking available in the RED LOT.

SM - Sidney Marcus Aud., Bldg. A
TM - Thomas Murphy Aud., Bldg. B
GA - Georgia Ballroom, Bldg. C

Maximize Your
Marketing Presence

Alicia

Marketing always involves a multi-pronged, intentional approach. Most churches need to look seriously at how to maximize their presence within their budgetary constraints. Considering all of the marketing resources and tools and ways that are out there to market, you need to ask the questions about where (e.g., text messaging, website, postcards, etc.) and how to invest your marketing dollars — whether you have $100 or $1,000 or $10,000.

Identify people in your congregation or in your social network and tap their expertise. Tap into those who attend your events or maybe some colleagues who know marketing, and just talk with them. If they're good, they'll ask things such as: Who is your target audience? What message do you want to convey? What type of budget do you have? Then based on that, what tactics are feasible? Together you can map out a plan. Putting a lot of thought into answering these questions up front can help you with planning and ensure effectiveness with your marketing efforts. We had short-term and long-term strategies, each with specific goals and marketing priorities.

When I came onboard, Olu was excited about billboards. As a marketing professional, I'm concerned when people want to invest in a billboard, because it often requires the majority of your marketing resources. I was reluctant about spending the entire budget on one billboard. I knew one marketing initiative would not be sufficient to cause people to begin rushing the doors. So we started smaller — with posters — and then expanded and grew from there.

As you are creating your plan, make sure you have a variety of mediums and messages that all have a consistent vibe and point people in the same direction. You do not want people to see the same billboard over and over again — they'll start tuning you out. You want people to see your name and brand in different places.

You need to ensure your marketing approach includes long-term replication and that your budget can sustain it. It takes multiple impressions, so don't get discouraged.

Also, try different ways of doing things so that you don't quickly give up after a tactic fails. Avoid throwing in the towel after you send one direct mail card and no one comes. Repeat, repeat, repeat! Long-term repetition is key.

People will feel in their subconscious that they are seeing you everywhere they go, in different places and in different ways (e.g., through friends/colleagues, billboard, email, social media, etc.). An integrated marketing plan will accomplish your goal in a shorter time for less money.

MAKE AN IMPACT!

Find a marketing expert or two who will help you create a plan that works within your budget, that is sustainable and that includes repetition.

Check out other churches, companies and organizations that have excellent marketing strategies and duplicate their approach/methods.

Engage Volunteers in Your Marketing Plan

Alicia

Even with a staff-level marketing person, that person needs to be supported by a large team of volunteers. Within our community, we are blessed to have a wide variety of marketing professionals. We have everything from public relations experts to writers to video production people. A dedicated group is also developing TV commercials. We have amassed so much talent and experience in filming, film editing, television and video production that our volunteer team is almost on autopilot. These proven professionals are able to create a storyboard and run with the concept. All of these skills are used by the marketing team to create an edgy, Impact vibe.

As a staff team lead, I discover what people want to do, what they're good at, and then encourage them to run with it. I seek to give them a sense that we aren't merely a team that meets and makes decisions. We're a team of owners who create. I let them know that if anyone has a great idea, the expectation is to make it happen; take ownership of it.

People are excited by the different creative designs and concepts that come out of marketing. Many of them still don't realize what it takes to produce that one great looking flyer, that one attention-grabbing advertisement. Marketing is hard work.

Different people on the team are active at different times, but they all contribute something. Although our volunteers have good public relations skills, they may not be available to take on a huge project. So I put together a detailed task list and ask people to pick a task. The task list strategy has been very successful. Because we have a lot of marketing profession-als, I understand the demand. People get busy. They have the best intentions, but they may not be able or capable of meeting the challenge. Furthermore, sometimes even the task list is overwhelming for people.

For example, I had one team member who kept saying she wanted to do something. When I asked her to select a task from the to-do list, nothing happened. So I changed my strategy and asked her to help me get a story into a certain newspaper. It had been on my list of "things to do" for a long time. I didn't have enough time to do it, but she did. Almost immediately, she reached out to the right person and booked the interview. Sometimes making a specific request is more effective than presenting a list of opportunities. In different seasons, different people are active and they come in at just the right time.

MAKE AN IMPACT!

Who do you need to engage as a volunteer on your marketing team? Construct your list of marketing "to do's." Don't be afraid to make specific requests of people.

Impact **◉ Idea 24** Empower Your Strongest Marketing Weapon

Edwin and Alicia

The strongest marketing weapon any church or organization has is its people — those who attend their events and/or worship experiences regularly. Before we had the marketing team up and running, word of mouth was one of our most powerful tools for growth. People told other people about their experience with great enthusiasm. As the person who leads marketing, I was drawn to Impact through word of mouth.

Leaders can encourage this marketing approach directly. Some places routinely ask folks to call another person and say, "Come to church." Impact didn't use that strategy, but we did seek to create that behavior as part of the DNA.

Instead of asking people to make calls, we created an environment where people *wanted* to invite others. We believe this strategy worked for two reasons: (1) Participants felt good enough about the experience to leverage their relationships; and (2) Participants believed that despite their level of spirituality, the person would benefit greatly from our worship experience/context. We used a "taste and see" marketing approach.

Another benefit of marketing this way is, IT IS FREE! Don't think you have to have a million dollars to have effective marketing. During a worship service, we encouraged people to pull out their cell phones in worship (almost everyone in our church has one) and text someone to invite them to church:

"Will you come to church with me on Sunday?" People got responses, and it was exciting to hear reports back even before worship was over. This is one example of a very simple tactic that made a big difference. We leveraged the relationships of our participants without writing a single check.

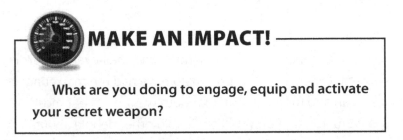

MAKE AN IMPACT!

What are you doing to engage, equip and activate your secret weapon?

Know Your Target Audience Personally

Olu and Alicia

One of the first things you have to do before you create a marketing plan is understand who you're seeking to reach. You must know who your target audience is.

What are they thinking about?

What motivates them?

What do their lives look like?

What are their beliefs?

What is important to them?

The answers to these questions will help you understand how to best communicate with or reach your target audience.

We understood we were reaching out to an audience that may not have experienced a church environment previously, or for some reason, had been chased out of church. A percentage really didn't like church. The target audience was a lot like Alicia, our first, paid marketing team leader. She shared how she felt before having an experience at Impact. This is her story:

Prior to coming to Impact, I had come to the conclusion that I didn't like church. I had been to several churches. I'd been to a big church, a small church, a traditional church, and a contemporary church. I did not like church. It was usually long, so I would go late…arrived in time for a song and a sermon. If the sermon was a little bit long, I'd be shifting in my seat thinking about how the time I was spending at church didn't seem worth all the bother.

When I started helping Impact, I used my personal experience as a springboard to understanding our target audience. A lot of

*people are turned off by church and turned off by religion, because
they see these images of divisiveness in the media and culture.
There's another segment of folks who are offended by those who
believe that if you don't go to church, you are going to hell. This
is not your best marketing message when you're trying to attract
people who have had very limited experience with church. Even if
some churches don't say it, they imply it. Some people feel con-
demned by those in the church if they don't attend church or if
they're not affiliated with a particular faith community.*

We conducted focus groups with samples from our target
audience. We asked questions about their attitudes towards
religion, faith, and spirituality. We discovered we had a lot of
people who consider themselves spiritual but not religious. For
them, "religious" meant too "rigid," and too many "rules."

It became clear, we needed to communicate that Impact
isn't about what you are doing right or what you are doing
wrong. It isn't about tradition or veiled expectations, such as
what you wear to church.

We wanted to create an environment where people felt a
sense of peace and freedom. We wanted them to feel totally
accepted. So we communicated that in the look and feel of
our materials and made sure that the verbal message wasn't
divisive, condemning, or judgmental. We also made sure that
the message was not rule-based; for example, telling people
they have to come every Sunday — no pressure.

We wanted our communications to be light-hearted to
counter-balance the notion that religion can be seen as very
serious business and set apart from the fun in life. We wanted
to share that our faith includes everything from humor, laughter and joy to sadness; the entire spectrum. We believe it is
important for us to communicate the entire spectrum because

people who aren't in our churches often only see the serious-ness of church, the rigidness of it, and the preachiness of it. The church experience should also give emphasis to laughter and the joy of serving God.

MAKE AN IMPACT!

Do you have people working on your marketing team who personally relate to your target audience? How have you sought to get to know your target audience personally? If you haven't done so already, commit to conduct at least one focus group to be sure you are on track.

Try a Logo-less Launch

Alicia, Olu, Edwin

The title of this idea alone may cause some church plant-ers out there to break into a cold sweat. Picture this: You've got three months left until the opening service. Or, you've got six months or a whole year, and OMG (Oh-My-God), there is no logo. You are biting your nails because someone from church planting school told you that if you don't have a logo, the church isn't going to work.

It is funny how much emphasis people place on the logo. And while a logo is important, in as much as it provides some-thing consistent that you could identify yourselves with, it is merely a part of the branding process — not the brand itself. As we mentioned before, it isn't only about branding a name. It is about creating a certain feel. Marty Neumeier pushes the whole branding concept to another level in his masterpiece *The Brand Gap*. Specifically he suggests the next level of corpo-rate logos will be "icons" and "avatars."[5] These are images and concepts that aren't static but are in motion. They are organic. Therefore, we recommend that you take the time needed to develop your logo, icon or avatar.

There was no logo when Alicia, our lead marketing person, was brought onboard. Other team leads expressed their con-cern. I think some people thought if we didn't have our logo, we were going to Hell.

Our logo emerged about nine months after Alicia came onboard, which was thirteen to fourteen months into Impact's lifespan. We were actually worshiping for about a year, logo free; and that was okay. We wanted a brand that was well thought out although we knew we weren't going to be married to it forever. Part of our DNA is that we're not stuck in one particular look or one particular environment. It was important to us that we have a dynamic logo. Dynamic means that it is something that can be applied in a variety of ways (colors, textures, etc.) or you may have different versions of the same logo. (This is in contrast to static logos that have the same red, black, green dot all the time in every place for 20 years.)

We took our time and explored our identity. The logo we came up with was based on feedback from the focus groups we conducted. We wanted to know what people were saying about Impact and how they heard about it. It was kind of a natural fit. The "I" in Impact is an exclamation mark on the final draft of the logo. When the designer proposed that to me, I said, "Hmm, that might work. When I went back over some of the focus group notes, I discovered that several people had expressed such a sense of excitement. That response was the confirmation we needed to move forward.

MAKE AN IMPACT!

The logo is only one component of the branding process. Take a look at your branding process and identify the one step that will most help you position your church or organization in your mission field or market.

Get a Social Media Plan

Edwin

We use social media at Impact to engage or communicate with our community. At Impact, communication is vital to our life existence. We are always striving to keep our community informed about what is going on and how they can connect with us or each other.

Let's take a look at Impact's communication continuum. This is a tool I use to show people how and where we make sure all of our communication is targeted. At Impact we try to reach our community in several different ways:

1. through social media,
2. on our website,
3. through e-mail , and
4. in worship.

As Impact's leader in the Communications arena, I always want to make sure we hit the social media realm with our update information first. When we are successful in getting our message out through social media we simultaneously hit our other forms of communication as well. Social media allows Impact to have a greater reach regarding with whom, when, and how information is shared. When left to their own devices, people often chose to start sharing information inside their walls during a weekend experience. This may have been the ultimate strategy before social media, but it would not be the wisest strategy today. At Impact, we are aware that there are more people who are not within the walls of the church throughout the week than there are who come to a weekend experience. We want to make sure all are aware of what's happening at Impact; therefore, the communication focus is both external and internal. This concept helps us spread the love of Christ to the world in a viral format. When a person receives a communication from Impact, it must be relevant and "cool" so that they are compelled to pass it on to others. In this way our communication becomes viral and reaches a higher number of people.

Impact uses three social media avenues to meet the needs of a growing demographic. We have a Facebook account, which consists of a Friend page and a Fan page. As of March 2011, more than 2,000 people have connected with us on Facebook and Twitter. We have a LinkedIn profile which is the preferred professional networking site. These platforms are highly interactive. They enable us to respond in real time to any inquires or comments. This interaction creates a sense of customer service with our community.

We have set up our Facebook and Twitter accounts to synchronize content automatically. If we post text and/or graphics on one, they automatically show up on the other. Linking these two platforms actually multiplies the number of persons within our community that receives our communication pieces.

The frequency of communications sent via these channels varies. Anytime we feel like we have something to share with our community, we send it.

I cannot over emphasize the relevancy and the reach that social media has helped Impact attain. These tools have brought to life the biblical message of taking the Gospel into all the highways and byways. The viral effect of these tools allows us to expand how we are creating and building relationships that spread the Gospel of Jesus Christ.

MAKE AN IMPACT!

If you haven't joined the social media communications stream, now is the time to take the plunge. Probably the easiest way to get started is to find someone who loves using social media (including Facebook and Twitter). Ask them to get you started. You may even end up recruiting them for the communications team!

Social Media Facts

Social media is a rapidly spreading phenomenon.

- By 2010, Generation Y will outnumber Baby Boomers; and 96% of them have joined a social network.[6]
- One out of eight couples married in the U.S. last year met via social media.[7]
- Facebook's adoption rate is blowing previous communications channels out of the water. Here's how long it took other innovations to reach 50 million users:
  - ◆ radio=38 years
  - ◆ TV=13 years
  - ◆ the Internet=4 years
  - ◆ iPod=3 years.

  Facebook added 100 million users in less than 9 months and the iPhone Facebook App hit 1 billion in 9 months.[8]
- If Facebook were a country, it would be the world's fourth largest between the United States and Indonesia. And it is still rapidly growing. Facebook recently announced 300 million users.[9]

The statistics above illustrate how differently our society is communicating with one another. Leaders at Impact have encouraged participation in this "new" communication game and see how these tools can help us get out into "all the world" and make disciples of Christ.

Impact Idea 28
Assess Marketing by Reach Not Attendance

Alicia

It is important to be clear about how we measure the success of our marketing strategy. Marketing measurements should capture how much we have broadened our effect, rather than how much we have increased our membership or attendance. We need to understand how we touch people, whether or not we are sparking their curiosity, and whether or not they recognize that they have heard discussions about us.

Additionally, we are also marketing to our active attendees. They need to be reminded of the vision of the church (doing church differently in our case) and of the brand they are promoting.

Measuring the number of first-time guests at our Sunday worship is important, but it doesn't go far enough. We need to try to measure how far our inspiration reaches. How far does it go — distance and depth from the church location? How far away were the respondents when they heard about Impact Church? Usually, I gauge our progress in terms of buzz. In other words, when I ask: "Have you heard of Impact Church," I'm looking for responses like: "Yeah, I think I've seen something about Impact… I don't know where. Wait, they have a billboard or website or something."

We measure depth by how accurate the respondents' impressions are of us. Do they communicate that Impact Church is a new church in the area "doing church differently?"

For us, marketing church differently helps us clarify the message with people. For example, when we were preparing to launch our second service, we sent teams to different locations such as shopping malls and grocery centers to hand out leaflets. Some of those teams did something extra — they helped people with their groceries while they distributed the flyers. As a result, people got the impression that we were there to help them — to make a difference. Even if the individuals who were helped never came to Impact, they might mention the gesture to someone looking for a church home.

Ultimately, it takes multiple impressions to stimulate someone to action. Many people require at least five or six impressions presented in five or six different ways before the impact is great enough for them to take action.

 **MAKE AN IMPACT!**

How are you measuring the success of your marketing? What new ideas do you want to try based on what you've read?

Small Groups

DRIVE TO REACH OUR GOD-GIVEN POTENTIAL

Get a Running Start

Anika

There are many ways to start a small group ministry. We share our approach as a springboard for your consideration.

We began by researching several models of doing small group ministry. We met with people and visited churches to learn how other organizations did small groups. We also began to envision Impact's hybrid model of small groups. We eventually named the ministry "Connection Groups."

Our Connection Groups are small gatherings of people who come together regularly to share with each other, grow spiritually, and help make the community and the world a better place. Our purpose is to empower people to connect with each other, build relationships, and realize their God-given potential; thereby, leading to transformed lives and stronger communities.

In the pre-launch phase, we formed two small groups made up of people who were on our advisory team (the team that was preparing to launch Impact). The purpose was to try out the process and identify people who could possibly serve as facilitators for the groups when we got them started. We selected a spiritually-based book, *Dream Giver*, by Bruce Wilkerson. It was a very simple book with a universal message that was appealing to everyone, regardless of their faith affiliation or non-affiliation. We wanted a very simple, engaging read to which people of all levels could relate. We especially wanted these groups to become a force that would draw people who were not necessarily a part of a church or who weren't used to being in church.

The groups met in homes. We rotated the locations of the groups, and we also rotated people who provided refreshments. Fellowship was an important part of the group during those early days. Eventually we even allowed a few people to take turns facilitating the sessions.

When we completed the book, we asked for volunteers to start the new Connection Groups: "Ok, who's interested in leading one of these? Who's willing to stand up and give this a try?" Enough people accepted the challenge to put our Connection Groups on the map.

 **MAKE AN IMPACT!**

If you don't yet have a small group ministry, who should be in your first one? If you do have a small group ministry, is it time to encourage some of the groups to spread and multiply?

Impact Idea 30
Connect People Through Small Groups

Anika and Olu

When Olu and I first met to discuss the vision that he had for Impact church, I was immediately drawn to the small group concept. The vision was an opportunity to meet people where they are; to tap into people's potential, help them recognize that potential, and grow from there. It was important to me that the groups represent not only the people who came to Impact, but also the community at large. Connecting the church and community has always been my passion. I was captivated by the idea of using small groups to reach people outside the church instead of trying solely to bring them into fellowship. The small group concept also helped church members reach out to the community.

Our Connection Groups (Impact's name for small groups) are doing a tremendous job helping us build relationships. A young woman who had just started coming to Impact decided that she wanted to commit to grow spiritually on her own without being directed by her parents. She immediately joined a Connection Group. She'd never been a part of any kind of Bible Study or anything spiritually based. But she joined a Connection Group. During those meetings she had an opportunity to share her dreams with group members, and they encouraged her and helped her in her walk of faith. As a result of her Connection Group experience, she was able and willing to venture forth and live a confident life. She has grown spiritually and she has learned how to use the gifts that God has given her. She received the assurance to use her gifts, and it has been a blessing, both to the Impact community and the larger community.

Another person was in the process of transitioning back into the Atlanta community. Through his Connection Group he found a community of people who supported him and helped him with the move. Since then he has become an active volunteer in all phases of Impact. Now he is leading a Connection Group himself.

Connection Groups help people identify their dreams and also realize them. Through that fulfillment, they get connected; not only with us at Impact but also with God and the community outside Impact.

 **MAKE AN IMPACT!**

What process do you have in your church that serves to build relationships with God and others so that people inside and outside your church are drawn in and fed?

Share — Don't Teach — in Small Groups

Anika

The only "qualifications" that we had for our Connection Group facilitators were for them to be:

1. committed and willing to serve,
2. open to learning themselves,
3. unafraid to make mistakes, and
4. willing to participate fully as a member of the group.

From the beginning, we did not want our small group of facilitators to be the "expert teachers" with an "I'm the teacher, you're the student," attitude. Instead, we wanted them to approach facilitating a Connection Group from the point of view that they were on a journey alongside the other group members. Finally, we wanted them to have participated in a group themselves. Our initial group of facilitators was diverse. They ranged from people who had never led anything in a church setting to people who were experienced Bible Study teachers.

I can remember one person from our initial pre-launch group who wanted to facilitate. He wanted to start a group because he felt that he had grown so much from participating in the pre-launch group. His whole life had been opened up, and he wanted to pass that experience on to others; but, he was afraid to facilitate because he had never taught Sunday School or Bible Study. Furthermore, he wasn't sure if he had enough knowledge to lead a small group.

We assured him that we weren't looking for traditional, experienced teachers. That is why we call the leaders "facilitators" and not teachers. We helped him to realize he was an expert on how his life had been impacted by working with the launch team and participating in the group, and this is what he could share with others.

We emphasized that the playing field was leveled with all of the facilitators — people were sharing, not teaching. We were sharing our experiences, encouraging and supporting each other, and also holding one another accountable.

Another person who was not already part of the launch team was motivated to join that pre-launch group. He just happened to be at one of the homes where we were having a session. Almost immediately, he developed a serious interest in Impact and Olu invited him to participate.

He enjoyed it so much that he attended all of the pre-launch sessions, became a committed volunteer at Impact, and was one of our initial facilitators.

Amazingly, men who have never taught a Sunday School class are facilitating some of our groups. This reaction is possible because we structured our groups as a sharing, not teaching, ministry. The fact that we're sharing our experiences together breaks down the wall that divides experts from novices and creates an environment that is full of possibilities.

MAKE AN IMPACT!

The higher the bar is set for small group facilitators, the slower and more difficult it will be for your groups to multiply. Take a look at whether or not shifting to more basic "facilitation" requirements might just be the missing spark!

Leverage Your Relationships

Impact Idea 32

Anika & Edwin

We encouraged facilitators and group members to invite people to participate whom they knew were not actively involved in a church or a faith community...family, friends, neighbors, and co-workers. We removed the expectation that people in a Connection Group had to come to Impact. That was the way we began to build the groups.

Initially, it was difficult for some. People resisted the idea of inviting non-Impact people. They'd say, "I only know the people who are here." And we would encourage them to think about others who are outside their initial comfort zone.

After continuous discussions amongst our team, each group was reminded of the initial purpose for the groups: to help people form relationships, to get them connected with each other; and together, begin to make an impact in their communities. We wanted an environment where everybody would be missed by somebody if they weren't around for a couple of weeks.

This type of accountability comes naturally in a setting where people are seeking to help one another make a difference, where group members have relationships outside of "church." After a person shares his or her God-given dream, you are compelled to see how they are doing. You may ask, "Have you been working on...?" or "What's the latest status with this project, with your business, with the organization, or with the ministry that you wanted to be involved in?" We wanted a place where people felt there was real intimacy...

where people felt comfortable enough, and safe enough to not only share their dreams, but to also give and receive constructive feedback. Sometimes church doesn't create a safe space where we can really let down our guard; to expose our places of struggle and receive encouragement. Connection Groups are places where healthy and positive accountability happens; where people are encouraged to submit to spiritual accountability with other people.

The chief purpose of our Connection Groups is not to produce Bible scholars. We want people who are grounded and growing, knowing who they are, building a closer relationship with God, and strengthening their relationships with each other. We want people to learn how to live their faith in the world, day by day, and we know that's a process. This connection does not happen while sitting in a class here or there. It is a day-by-day process. It's a process that requires encouragement as well as guidance and openly shared stories in order to grow.

 **MAKE AN IMPACT!**

How might you encourage people to leverage their relationships? Does anything about your current small group process create barriers to that? If so, remove them!

Impact Idea 33
Take Yourself to the World
Olu

When we envisioned this whole Connection Group process, we understood it to be an evangelistic process; a process we would use to reach different cultures. With that in mind, we understood the need for multiple avenues that introduced people into the life of the church. This is why we made the Sunday School model obsolete in the Impact Church model.

I don't want to imply that having Sunday School is a terrible thing. However, if we had done Sunday School initially, it would have been more internal than external. We've got multiple Connection Groups that aren't meeting inside a church building. They are meeting in coffee shops. They are meeting in homes. They are meeting throughout the metropolitan area of Atlanta, Georgia. Soon we will have web-based Connection Groups that will allow people all over the world to connect. It is a tremendous blessing when we see photos of individual Connection Group experiences — we are introduced to faces we've never seen before.

Some people who go to Connection Groups may not come to weekend worship. Other people go to Connection Groups first, and then to weekend worship, which means we see new faces all the time. Multiple avenues of fellowship make it possible for Impact church to connect with new people in exciting ways.

In the initial round of groups we had someone who joined a Connection Group who was not even a Christian. He came because he enjoyed the camaraderie and the conversation, and that is the whole purpose of the groups. Likewise, groups are gathering in public places, like restaurants and coffee shops, where it is natural for people to drop in. And others meet in homes in different communities. There are people who will come to a group because they may be visiting someone, or they may be in the area. One of our groups meets in a subdivision clubhouse. One night a woman joined the group meeting in the subdivision thinking she was sitting in on the neighborhood association meeting. At some point, I'm sure she realized this wasn't the association meeting, but she enjoyed it so much she stayed to the end and asked if she could join the group.

We want to connect with people. Our format is to take ourselves to the world.

 **MAKE AN IMPACT!**

In what consistent ways are you taking your congregation to the world? What are you currently doing that could be re-designed to take your congregation to the world more strategically?

Oh, My God (OMG), No Sunday School!

Impact launched as a hybrid: we had a worship component and a small group component (our Connection Groups). We had no Sunday school, no Bible studies, and no youth group.

We may have upset some who can't conceive of a church without either of those. Some may have been thinking "If you don't have a Sunday School, then everybody's probably not gonna make it into Heaven." What we're discovering is, there are different formats, whether for planting churches or for existing churches, that don't necessarily have a Sunday School product, but people can still be taught and learn and graduate to the next level.

Create Demand

Anika and Edwin

Creating demand for small groups is about building momentum and maintaining excitement. Initially, quite a few people expressed an interest in Connection Groups--many more than we expected. We recognized the unique opportunity to continue encouraging and building this concept.

Here are some examples of how we seek to create demand.

1. Meet every other week instead of every week. This schedule allows people to rest and do other things in between, while still keeping the continuity. In this format people are ready to come; they're looking forward to the next group.

2. Limit the number of sessions (from six to eight sessions) instead of allowing the groups to go on indefinitely. Initially, the reason we did that was to examine how these groups worked; to stop, review, assess, and make modifications as needed. We then realized we were onto something.

3. Mix groups demographically (gender, age and marital status) in the early phases so everybody feels like there is a group they could go to and not feel like: "Oh, I can't be in this group." We wanted to increase the options people had so if they found a group that fit their time and location they could go without limitations. Although in year two, we started adding age-level groups (e.g., youth), the majority of our groups remain mixed.

4. Expect duplication. Groups are expected to divide at the end of each session. This notion of duplicating is built

into most small group models. However, our model asks groups to divide after a relatively short period. We ask groups to re-form after about three months and that's not the easiest thing. In many cases groups were growing closer bonds with each other and with God and wonderful things were happening.

In Impact's infancy, we wanted as many people as possible to be able to become a part of this experience, to get connected. The only way we could do that is by continuing to reach out and divide. Even though we encounter problems and some resistance from groups reluctant to divide and duplicate, we press on. Since the majority of Connection Group participants end up being involved in other aspects of Impact, we can assure them that they would be able to continue to stay connected with one another in other capacities.

While it can be painful for people to build relationships only to be "encouraged" to part or end the group, this practice creates a demand for fresh relationships and for new Connection Group experiences.

 **MAKE AN IMPACT!**

Which strategy for creating demand for your small groups will you try? What modifications do you need to make, given your context? Is there another strategy that is emerging for you?

By the end of 2009, 400 people participated in small group experiences via Impact Church

Impact Idea 35

Make Getting Started in a Connection Group Fun and Stress-Free

Anika

We throw a party before the launch of a new session of Connection Groups. (We learned to call it a "spread party" from Andy Stanley at North Point Community Church.) We throw a reception after the worship experiences, invite people to come and meet the facilitators and sign up for a group. We get our largest number of people at these events. Additionally, all facilitators and team members are intentional about making sure every potential Connection Group member gets at least one touch.

After signing up for a group, the participant receives a call or email from the facilitator at least once before the start of the group. The participant learns all of the logistical details (e.g., date, time, location, host names, etc.). Then, he or she receives a reminder a day before the first session. Participants receive great food at the Connection Group sessions. Food is important. It is a universal barrier breaker. The remainder of the initial session is a time for getting to know one another. It is intended to be comfortable and establish an atmosphere conducive to sharing.

We have people who come to Impact who make a personal decision to rededicate their lives to Christ. Often these people join Connection Groups to focus on their spiritual development. Yet, people who are new to the faith or who are returning after a break, are often a little afraid about going to a group. They may have bad memories about Bible Study or

Sunday School and/or they may feel uncomfortable with their level of Biblical understanding.

When they come to the Connection Group, they immediately feel at home. They see other people like them are there learning and growing and wanting to share. They also feel at home because they recognize that they are going to be appreciated and valued for who they are. These are the things that are important to people.

We have discovered it is far better for people to be drawn into groups rather than "shamed" into groups. People who have participated in Connection Groups on their own rather than us having to "preach to them" or twist their arm with "you ought to do this" or "you should change this about your life" are much more likely to stick with it.

When people are drawn into the groups and are around people who are living their life and living their faith differently as a result of the group, the conditions are ripe for transformation. In this climate, people think, "I want to do something different with my life; I want to change." When that revelation comes for them, you know it's real.

 **MAKE AN IMPACT!**

What two things can you do to increase the fun and decrease the stress of joining a small group and going to its first meeting?

Train for Support and Engagement

Edwin and Anika

We try to meet with Connection Group facilitators regularly to nurture, encourage, and support them. We do this because they are facilitating on a volunteer basis, and many of them have never done anything like this before. Everyone at Impact, especially a member of a Connection Group, knows that you've got to step outside your comfort zone if you are going to grow and live the life God intends for you.

Whenever people are facing new experiences at Impact, we try to provide as much support as possible for them, offering suggestions, talking with them about how things are going, and providing materials.

All of our facilitators come to the training having experienced membership in a Connection Group. Now we've asked them to step into the facilitator role and many are afraid because they are out of their comfort zone. So we put all facilitators through a half-day orientation/training event prior to the start of a new Connection Group session.

Training starts out with food...food is important! The training sessions are held in the morning and they last about four hours. After a continental breakfast, we'll do an engaging icebreaker activity to warm people up and get them on the road to sharing and learning more about each other. We also incorporate some experiences or activities that help people discern a little bit more about themselves. These insights may be about their leadership style or their work style.

After the warm-up icebreaker, we give them an overview of what the Connection Groups are; we share our vision of small groups of people working in relationship with each other to reach out and spread the love of Christ within their communities. And then, we usually have some activity that is interactive. We don't lecture them.

We get them involved in participatory activities that give them an opportunity to practice some of the things they'll be doing in the group. For example, we may give them a section from the book they're going to read and put them in a small group for a facilitation-related activity. As a group, they may have 10–15 minutes to develop a presentation on how they would share the theme of this particular chapter.

They are up; they're moving; they're in groups. They're acting things out. Experience and research have shown that people learn best and remember the most when they have been actively involved in the learning process.

MAKE AN IMPACT!

How are you equipping and feeding your small group leaders? Are you touching the whole learner? What ideas have you gotten for improving your training event?

A Quick & Simple Training Icebreaker

Have everyone line up in two lines facing each other and give them a series of questions or subjects to share with each other. "You have 30 seconds to share something with the person standing opposite you." It could be something about yourself; it could be a question you have to answer about your interests. After 30 seconds we yell "next," and everyone moves on to the next person. It is sort of like speed dating without the awkwardness.

Go through the exercise until everyone has had a chance to interact with each other. This activity gets the energy going! You learn things about people that you wouldn't have learned otherwise.

Keep It Fresh

Olu, Anika, and Edwin

The great secret to these Connection Groups is that although we have more than twelve Connection Groups meeting at any given session, not one group is facilitated by the lead pastor. While he attends a Connection Group experience along with Edwin and their families, he doesn't lead one. That was the design from the beginning, and we appreciate one of his coaches for helping him understand that he had to move out of the way.

Of course, the lead pastor makes sure the groups don't go AWOL or become mutants of the vision. If you can find a great and gifted leader who has oversight over the process, who has a theological understanding and cares about people, you will succeed.

We have sought to repeat that pattern on a small and large scale with our facilitators. For example, after our facilitators have led for a couple of sessions, we ask them to sit back and encourage someone else to facilitate. We need breaks to not only get a rest and be rejuvenated, but to also keep it fresh. As an added benefit, we identify new potential small group leaders.

We asked our founding set of facilitators to take a rest after they had been facilitating for a year. That's something that we will always encourage people to do so that we have fresh energy flowing within our Connection Groups.

It is easy for servants of the Lord to find themselves in perpetual serving mode; working, but not taking care of ourselves.

We have to take care of our bodies, minds, hearts, spirits — we have to stop for a second and take care of ourselves.

One reason for Impact's rapid growth is we continually encourage others to take ownership of their Connection Group. This strategy minimizes burn-out and maximizes talent.

MAKE AN IMPACT!

How do you encourage your leaders to rest and rejuvenate? Is it intentional or only in case of an emergency?

Got fresh growth?

Impact Idea 38

Grow New Small Group Models to Overcome Challenges

Anika

While God has blessed our small group ministry mightily, we are still perfecting it, and it is still evolving. Initially, our goal was to keep the groups small, between 8-12 people, but that hasn't always happened. Keeping the groups small hasn't always happened because we didn't have enough facilitators and because some days are more popular than others (there are just certain days when people prefer to attend a group).

In our first round, we continued to add people throughout the course of the session, because we wanted everybody to be in a group. That meant that we might have had people entering the group even towards the end of a session. After two

---

Share and Multiply Leadership

We have found that the majority of the people who participated in those Connection Groups ended up becoming involved in some other area of Impact. We quickly realized Connection Groups was an active avenue into the life of the Church.

Part of our model is that after a couple of sessions, the initial facilitators encourage others in the group to step up and try their hand at facilitation. In doing so, we begin to identify who, potentially, may be a facilitator for the next round.

---

years of this model, we changed it because the groups found it disruptive. Now we stop allowing people to sign up for a group after the second meeting or after the group reaches a certain size (whichever comes first). For those who come late to the sign-up process, we either ask them to wait until the next enrollment period or, if there are enough people waiting to get into a small group, we may form a new one.

Our primary goal is to provide quality training for our people so they are able to grow. The challenge has been to find time and not overburden people. Many of our facilitators are also involved in other areas of leadership at Impact. Generally, if we don't put some boundaries around volunteer time commitments, people will go and go and go and do until they get tired. Then they fall out of the loop, and you don't see them anymore. We don't want that to happen. Currently we are working to have more facilitators who are not involved in any other area of leadership in the life of Impact.

MAKE AN IMPACT!

What challenges are you having with your small group ministry? What new models are you prepared to try in order to overcome those challenges?

Small Group Recap

1. You've already got what you need right there within your community. If you focus on helping people discover what they already have within themselves, if you help them find the confidence and the encouragement to live and act on the gifts they already have, you're way ahead — you're more than half way there.

2. Involve the people in your church or in your community in helping develop and build the process. Always remember the principle of spreading and sharing. Each one, teach one.

3. Continue learning and helping and building. Ministry is an ongoing process. When we stop growing, we begin to die. Therefore, we have to continue to learn.

Hospitality

DRIVE TO RADICAL CUSTOMER SERVICE

Hospitality is Your First Line of Defense

Sakon and Alan

Hospitality sets the tone for what is to come; as such, it is our first line of defense. We strongly suggest that you plan hospitality activities thoughtfully and thoroughly. At Impact we have two distinct welcoming teams: the Hospitality and Host Teams. The Hospitality Team ensures courtesy inside the building. The Host Team promotes courtesy outside the building.

We are the first Impact representatives that people see when they come to our church. If we stand at the front door with our arms folded, chewing gum, ignoring people who are walking by, or if we are off in our own world, people may be turned off by our appearance or behavior. It is similar to going to a four-star restaurant where the expectations are high, but the service is lousy. You have heard the food is exceptional and you just can't wait to eat it; but when you enter the dining area, nobody acknowledges you. It takes forever for you to be seated, and your waiter doesn't even come back to ask if you need more water or coffee. Would you bother going back to that restaurant even though the food was tremendous? Probably not.

The most important aspect of hospitality is "who" is serving. While logistics, creative use of space, planning and follow-up are important, the people serving in these areas are the ones who influence worshipers to return. Choose people who are flexible in their thinking, because they can prevent or manage conflict. Place people in areas where they can perform best. Appoint hospitality team members who are approachable flexible and open, not dictatorial. In other words, choose team members who don't need to have their own way all the time.

Pick people who are welcoming, who are inclusive in their manner and in their speech. As a pastor and a leader, use your common sense and spirit of discernment to recognize people who work well with others. Look for people who are bubbly, outgoing, accommodating, and creative — those with a desire to serve others and a willingness to do anything to make somebody else's experience great. It is better to have a smaller group of the right people than to have a larger group that includes people without these characteristics.

Creative Solutions Required in Non-Traditional Spaces

You have to be creative when you're operating in a multi-purpose space setting.

We struggled to hand out offering envelopes and pens as more and more people crowed through our doors. In a permanent worship space those items are typically placed in racks on the backs of pews or chairs, but in our setting we had to think creatively: "What can we do to make this setting better for those who are coming?" We needed something on the back of each seat to hold materials, so we went to a local home building store and bought aprons — the kind that you'll often see carpenters wear — and wrapped those around each seat. Carpenter aprons became the holders for our pens and paper materials. This adjustment is an example of how we seek to create an environment of radical hospitality. While activities like this may be time consuming, they matter.

Our focus on hospitality is similar to one of the principles of Chick-fil-A, Inc. founded by Truett Cathy. During a rough time in the formative years of the company, he and the executive team held a retreat to review the company's progress and make critical decisions about the future of the company. The ultimate blessing from the meeting was a corporate purpose statement. One of the statements is a principle that aligns with Impact. The statement is: "To have a positive influence on all who come in contact with Chick-fil-A." Mr. Cathy's commitment to focusing on leaving a positive impression on people translates to the church and other service organizations. It should be the goal of every service organization to make a positive impression on everyone with whom it comes into contact.[10]

MAKE AN IMPACT!

List those persons who came to mind as you were reading this chapter. Are they serving in a high-volume, high-touch and highly visible ministry like hospitality?

If you have already launched or are in an existing church, are there any people serving as greeters who resemble the service mentioned in the four-star restaurant story?

Based on your answers to the above questions, make the needed changes so your hospitality shines.

Become an Irresistible Welcoming Force

mpact Idea 40

Sakon

Hospitality is about letting everybody know that they are truly welcomed. It is about making everybody feel that their presence matters, regardless of the way they look, where they come from, how they are dressed.

We ask questions like: "Do you need something?" and "Can we help you?" before anyone asks us. One of our big goals is to provide RADICAL hospitality: providing great customer service to everybody that comes through the door.

As a team we "come as we are" (some people wear jeans, some people wear suits) so we can treat guests to the church as we would treat guests in our home. We are more relaxed and approachable. Add to that our outgoing personalities, and we become an irresistible welcoming force!

It is so important for those on the Hospitality Team to be outgoing, to be welcoming, to have open body language and to engage actively and seek people out. This is especially important for people who are newer on the scene and who may not have connected with anyone. Asking questions that demonstrate you care and that you have paid attention goes a long way toward creating an environment of radical hospitality. For example, "How are you doing today? Oh, I don't see your kids, how are they? Where are they?" or, "How was your surgery/trip/job interview?"

That type of radical hospitality — creating the experience of being known and being warmly approached as such — is something people look for and crave. Think about your favorite store;

the one you frequent all the time. You expect the sales person to recognize you and say, "Hey, Sakon! How was that green sweater I picked out for you? Did you like it? Did it work well?"

 **MAKE AN IMPACT!**

Nordstrom is often cited as an example of a company that provides the ultimate in customer service, and for good reason. Wal-Mart greeters provide another example of what radical hospitality looks like with their ready smiles, eye contact, stickers and shopping cart reverse-valet service at each entrance.

What is one thing you can do to improve your customer service so your hospitality will be more radical?

Hospitality Begins Before the Front Door

Alan

Our vision for outdoor hospitality goes far beyond setting up the parking, setting up the grounds, and marking out the special assistance parking. I think the most critical part of what we do outdoors is to keep it fresh, and try to make a lasting impression each and every week. We want to be that amazing glimpse of what people have in store for them at Impact that day.

Edwin calls us the pioneers because we are out in the elements — even when it's raining, cold or scorching hot — forging new paths. We get to the church around 6:00 a.m. to set up and to get ourselves ready to be radically hospitable in the parking lot. For us, that includes waving and smiling at everyone who drives in. We want to make sure that people come in refreshed. Even if they drive in with a lot of stuff on their minds, we ensure they are greeted with a smile and someone to help them transition to worship. We are there to help get the baby out of the car, or do whatever they may need. We want to be the answer for any issue they are having at that moment.

Our team is made up of dedicated people who are adaptable, open and have an attitude of "whatever-it-takes" service. We have a plan for how to direct people so that parking is more efficient, but we can't put that plan before God. If someone wants to park in a spot, as long as it's not a hazard to someone else's safety, we're not going to argue with them about it. We want them to come in and experience Impact, not get bent out of shape because we asked them to move or park in a less desirable spot.

As we greet people in the parking lot, we seek to cast a vision of what we are trying to do at Impact. It is great when we see someone, distracted by his or her own parking issues, come to realize that the parking lot represents something bigger than their issue; that the order and atmosphere of the parking lot matters. Eventually, people catch it. We try to stay focused on serving, teaching and making suggestions instead of simply directing traffic.

At Impact, things are evolving; things are changing, and we are always looking for a better way to do something. We say we are doing church differently, and we are changing the game. The "but we've always done it this way" mentality is widespread; and that attitude has no place at Impact.

Our constant improvement mindset requires people on the team to be very open minded and very flexible. People on the team offer suggestions; we talk about them, and a new approach is born. We all see the value of being open and listening. Everyone is on board with this methodology. I come from a process-improvement background. Naturally, Impact was a perfect opportunity for me to say, "Let's put everything on the table and see how we can do things differently in church moving forward."

MAKE AN IMPACT!

Where does (or where will) your hospitality minis-try start? Do you need to organize some pioneers?

Be Smooth and Fluid

Alan

During our initial launch planning, an image caught hold that continues to stimulate our thinking and shapes our activities. It was a picture of a drop of water falling into a body of water with ripples rolling out from the point of entry

The Impact Team wants to be that drop of water: fluid and flowing with whatever people may bring to the river of our common existence. We know that we came to the river with our own concerns and others may also have issues in their lives. We want the love of God to flow into them and through them so that the rest of their experience at Impact — and beyond Impact — will reflect the love of God.

We can be that flash point. We can be that drop of water that cascades the love of God throughout their lives on any given Sunday, and any given day. We know the message that's going to be delivered is going to do likewise, but we want to start them off right. We want people to say, "Hey, someone just smiled at me and said, "Hello," and when they said, "Hello" to me, they were really saying, "I love you; how's your day going?" So when people enter the worship experience, everything just flows.

Ideally, we want all operations, including outdoor hospitality, to run smoothly and in fluid fashion. We interact with people who are going through various situations and experiencing a range of moods on any given Sunday. As a servant leader it is helpful to focus on being fluid and smooth like that drop of water.

My advice is to trust God and "lean not on your own under-standing." Things aren't going to be perfect. Things are going to happen and you have to trust God.

That includes also trusting that God will challenge the people around you to do the things that they should do. Even though you can't make people do anything, ultimately you are responsible; and sometimes there are hard decisions that you have to make about who's to serve and in what role. In the end, you must allow people to walk their own paths with God. God will certainly deal with them and their circumstances. Trust God that everything is going to be okay.

MAKE AN IMPACT!

What image do you have in mind that helps you communicate what a smooth, fluid process looks like? If you don't have one, brainstorm one. If you do have one, evaluate whether it is helping your leaders understand the role they play and the result of the systems they are creating.

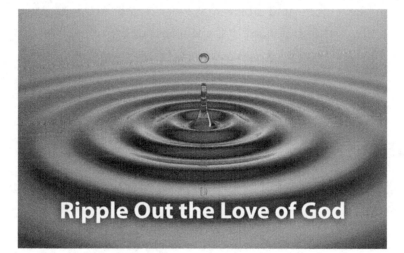

Ripple Out the Love of God

Impact Idea 43 Outdoor Hospitality is More Than Parking Cars

Alan and Edwin

The Host Team is concerned about more than putting a car in a spot and greeting the people who are heading into worship. Given that Impact is located near downtown Atlanta (a highly-populated urban area), we experience heavy foot traffic outside our worship space on Sunday morning. We encounter a lot of people who aren't on their way into our worship experience.

We have an active ministry to homeless people, addicted people and other wanderers whom we encounter when we're outside of the church. While most of the Impact folks are inside in the worship experience, we're engaging people on the outside who may be walking by and thinking, "What in the world is going on over here? Where did all these cars come from?"

We are seeking to create partnerships and connections by offering services that expand our ministry to the homeless. For example, we volunteer annually with Hosea's Feed the Hungry, a homeless initiative in Atlanta, Georgia. Our hope is that one day we can position ourselves to provide emergency and pro-active care for our homeless brothers and sisters as well.

So inside and outside the building on Sunday morning we are reaching the un-churched or the de-churched in unique, unexpected and creative ways.

MAKE AN IMPACT!

Many new church meeting spaces are not church-related and are actually spaces that are vacant on the weekends (e.g., office parks, schools, warehouse space, etc.). In these instances, people notice something different when this weekday-use space suddenly has a bunch of cars and/or activity surrounding the worship service on a weekend.

What are the ways you can use this outdoor buzz surrounding your worship service to increase your reach to those un-churched or de-churched in your community?

Make Time to Develop Hospitality Leaders

Impact Idea 44

Sakon

If you attract the right type of leaders to your hospitality ministry, they have specific needs that must be met in order to stay motivated. They need to feel the warm fuzzies, too. I seek to create this environment for my team by planning dinners, a fun event or two like bowling, and by personal check-ins. I call once or twice during the week to touch base and ask: "How are you doing?" I call to see how they are doing, because everyone wants to feel that they're appreciated and recognized for doing a good job. If I need to ask them a question about their role as a hospitality member or an agenda item, I make a separate call. It is very important to make at least one call a week to say, "I'm here and I care about you." This strategy helps build a dedicated team of volunteers who "get it."

I also believe it is essential to have team development meetings. These meetings are structured so that people will grow in their capacity to problem-solve, to be better hospitality folks and to increase their ownership of the ministry. We meet monthly to get everyone's ideas for improving the ministry on the table. I view this as an essential component for not only improving the ministry, but also for developing leaders. During the meetings I ask: What's working? What's not working? What can we keep the same? What should we change?

As the leader of the hospitality ministry, it is important to listen and take the time to clarify and note ideas and specifics. The leader should also keep track of people's growing edges and strengths.

Keep track of the types of duties, and what people's roles and responsibilities are. This plan of action prevents confusion and chaos when people come out to serve. Update roles and responsibilities documents as improvements are made to your hospitality process and also keep track of who may be ready to assume more responsibility.

 **MAKE AN IMPACT!**

How are you leading and developing your volunteers? Which of the ideas mentioned above will you commit to implementing?

Show 'Em You Care

Duplicate Yourself

Sakon and Edwin

Sakon's situation may sound familiar:

Leading the Hospitality Team can be overwhelming. I'm a school teacher and I found myself managing the ministry during break time and lunch time. I became accustomed to sending out emails, making telephone calls, and sending text messages in the midst of my daily routine. After doing this for a while, I reached a point where I realized I needed to get some help. I recruited about four other people who helped me during the week by following up with other people. Their help has made my job a whole lot easier. We talk at least two or three times a week to see what is needed to support the upcoming experience: What do we need for this event? How are things going? Who are we going to call? In addition to being responsible for the actual weekend hospitality function, we are responsible for the offering envelopes, supplies for the church (e.g., tissues). A whole lot goes into the hospitality process; it is more than just getting there in the mornings, greeting people and then going home.

Duplication is extremely important. We need to continually train and prepare new leaders. We need to duplicate what we do and who we are. If you are doing everything yourself, then you are probably not growing. If you are growing under these conditions, it is probably not a healthy growth process. We should intentionally train volunteers and equip them to take the ministry, the team, the area to the next level.

This can be difficult on many levels. Sometimes volunteers take more ownership than is healthy. They may have an attitude that conveys: "Hey, this is mine; this is what I do; this is how it's going to be until I decide I want to leave." What we're trying to communicate to all of our team leaders is that the best way to lead is to be a servant first. We call them "servant leaders" for that very reason.

On other occasions, people want to share responsibilities, but don't know how or don't have a clear goal or plan for doing so. We encourage leaders to identify task hand-off goals. For example, a leader may be doing task 1, task 2, task 3 and task 4 this month but his or her goal, by the end of month is to perform only task 1 and task 2. He or she should delegate tasks 3 and 4 to someone else. We believe that both the principle and the practice of task hand-off goals help all our teams grow.

At every team lead meeting, we express the message of and urgency around duplication. Each time someone said, "You've got to duplicate yourself!" Sakon would lower her head. She was thinking, "They're talking about me," and we could tell she felt a little sad about it. On several Sundays, we noticed that Sakon was overdoing it. We'd go up to her and say, "Sakon, you need to take a break. The only way that you're going to be healthy is for you to take a break." Nearly a year passed before she transitioned from doing the ministry to letting go and managing the entire team. Once that transition happened, we saw growth in the team.

MAKE AN IMPACT!

How are you encouraging team leaders to dupli-cate themselves? What is working? What isn't? If you are just starting out, try modeling the task hand-off goal principle and see what happens!

What task hand-offs do you need to practice?

Impact Idea 46
Address Volunteer Issues Head On
Sakon

Leading a team of volunteers can be a difficult undertaking. In a new church start like ours, the biggest challenge has been working with many different personalities and scheduling requirements.

I have learned four strategies for working with old-school and new-school personalities and would encourage you to try them on for size:

1. Approach each person with an open mind. In our context we work with people from all backgrounds and cultures. No one is the same. I have discovered that I need to learn how to relate to each person individually; that I can't talk to or communicate the same way with everyone. One volunteer may like to discuss things on the phone, while another prefers to talk in person immediately following the worship experience.

2. Enhance your listening and communication skills. This means listening without talking, being mindful of your body language, talking about the positives and suggesting ways to improve, etc. I had to learn how to talk to people so that I didn't come off as being hard or harsh. At times, I gave the wrong impression when giving directives — our volunteers do not like being told what to do. So instead of telling them what to do, I got a better response when I encouraged them. Constructive communication is VERY important.

3. Be approachable and open so that people will feel comfortable when talking to you and observing the way you interact with others.
4. Get to know the people who are working with you. This means communicating with them outside of church. Find out more about their likes and dislikes, their hopes and dreams, their victories and struggles. Express genuine interest in their families and friends. Engage in meaningful and thoughtful conversations to build rapport and team loyalty.

Conflicts in scheduling add to the interesting dynamics that accompany intergenerational or multi-cultural leadership. The people who sign up don't always show up. They will say, "Yes! I want to serve," but there is no follow-through. At times 15 people will sign up, but only four people will actually show up. I used to subdivide tasks so that each person had a clear role. However, I decided it would be wiser to schedule fewer people who do multiple roles than to schedule many people with individual roles.

At this point, I schedule the minimum number of people needed to serve per Sunday. This has helped clarify the need for these people — a few, not a team, are responsible. I also assign a volunteer to be on standby or serve as a backup.

Be flexible. Life happens and people can't always keep commitments. Things don't always go as planned. Always be ready to adjust and think quickly on your feet.

MAKE AN IMPACT!

What have you found to be your biggest challenges in leading a team of volunteers? What do you need to do to address them head on?

Everyone Communicates Differently: Match Communication Strategy to an Individual

We're technologically driven. We use texting and email extensively, but we understand that people relate to things differently. Some people can process instructions given through technology — they follow these instructions and they're on base. Some people are visual people. And some people simply can't get it unless they are talking it through. Think about those people who you go back and forth with on an email 10-20 times and you realize they're just not getting it. That's when you have to understand that YOU have to change the modality of your communication. In this instance, pick up the telephone, talk to them or meet face-to-face so that you can get on the same page. Make note of their communication preference so that you make an immediate communication connection next time.

Impact Idea 47 Find People Called to Serve Wherever the Need Is

Sakon and Alan

Certain types of people are needed during the initial stages of "planting" a church. Visionaries will do whatever needs to be done to support the dream. They feel called to serve. Impact is blessed to have persons on board who respond positively to ministry opportunities.

Sakon, our first Hospitality Team lead, describes her experience:

For several months, I had been praying to God because I felt a strong desire to serve. I knew I wanted to serve a ministry but didn't know which one, didn't know how, and I didn't know where God was going to put me. All I knew was that I wanted to serve. So I called Edwin and he asked me which area of ministry I felt called to serve. I told him that it didn't matter to me… wherever help was needed. He told me that Hospitality was the number one choice for me and I said, "Okay, I am ready." I didn't know what I was going to do or how I was going to do it, or when I was going to do it; but I knew I was ready to try. Later, I discovered that as soon as Edwin heard my bubbly and cheery voice, he immediately knew they had found their Hospitality leader.

Alan, our first Host Team lead, tells his story:

My journey to Impact started in the fall of 2006, when we were setting up to launch. My wife and I had several meetings with Olu and others who were going to be involved in the launch of Impact. We caught a glimpse of the vision and we were really excited about coming to Impact and being part of this new church start. When we came over, we didn't know that we would love it the way we do. We thought maybe we would come over for a while to help launch and that we would eventually go back to our original church. However, when we got here, we discovered it to be such a unique opportunity to serve God. Initially, I came on board just helping out wherever I could, helping to set up production, helping wherever I could make a difference. So far, the outdoors hospitality ministry (Host team) has proven to be a surprisingly fulfilling transition for me.

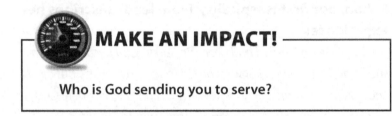

MAKE AN IMPACT!

Who is God sending you to serve?

Volunteer Ministry Leaders

At the outset most of our volunteer leaders had other full-time jobs. Leading a ministry can be especially challenging for volunteers because they have other commitments and because leading a ministry is a big responsibility.

For them to step up and play this role means that they are sacrificing some "free" time that they could devote to other activities. For example, our Outdoor Host leader, Alan, is a business consultant by profession, which means that he must be on the road during the week. Effecting change while he is out of town means making phone calls, begging and pleading with other people to handle something during the week if he can't. He tries to deal with vendors directly to maintain a single point of contact and build relationships (e.g., if we need to get a sign replaced or speed brakes, cones, etc.). He can't really do everything necessary to expand the ministry — meet with team members, work on projects, recruit, etc. — while he's out of town. This is another reason why it is critical to have a strong team that is committed to the purpose and vision of the ministry.

Move People So They Might Serve Productively

Max and Olu

If you have spent any time with a volunteer-driven organization, you have likely experienced a volunteer with a heart of gold who is totally out of place. Sometimes we tiptoe around the fact that somebody may be out of place. As a result, the person stays in a servant leadership role that is wrong for them for too long. I think we get stuck in this pattern because we aren't sure how to transition the individual to a better role.

The best thing that you can do for volunteers is to listen to them. We have found that people often come to serve with certain notions about what they want to do or what they are good at doing; but in reality, their ideas are neither the things they do best, nor the things that God wants them to do in order to strengthen the body of Christ.

When people are volunteering, they are often exploring what may be next for them. They may look at the list of options and say, "Production. That's what I want to do." All the while, they have no clue about what production is. In addition to hearing what they want to do, it is important for them to understand who they are in a broader context so you can help them discern what other areas they might try.

Not only do you need to listen to your volunteers, but you must also be able to give them honest feedback. You should not leave someone in a place where they are not being productive. Being truthful is the kindest thing you could do, because whether they realize it or not, they are not as happy as they would be serving in a position where they can use their natural gifts. Volunteering in a place where we aren't meant to serve increases the likelihood of burn-out, frustration, or system failure.

At Impact, we state the truth with love. We encourage volunteers to see their gifts and to understand that God has equipped each of us differently to play particular roles in the body of Christ. We empower them to make better choices about how to use their God-given gifts and talents. If necessary, we move people to a new volunteer position, and we encourage them to shine in other areas of ministry.

Legendary coach and team builder, Joe Gibbs writes, "Pick the right people and put them in the right jobs … Successful team-builders develop a knack for recognizing the right people for the right jobs. They then train and equip those people to use their God-given gifts and talents for the good of the team."[11] The direction of the ministry is tied to having the right people in the right places. If we believe that everyone has a seat on some bus (or a particular role to play in the Body of Christ), how can we drag our feet when it comes to repositioning people? The conversation about moving can be more positive since all we are trying to do is to find the right seats for all of us. You may be sitting in someone else's seat. Building relationships is essential throughout the process of making seat changes. This way the volunteer who is asked to change seats will understand that the request is grounded in love and appreciation.

MAKE AN IMPACT!

Identify one volunteer this week who you believe is in the wrong area. Who is the best person to shepherd this person into the right area? Connect the identified volunteer with the shepherd and ask the shepherd to work the process.

Worship

DRIVE TO WORSHIP CREATIVELY

It's About the Energy, Not the Weather

Edwin

Our first worship experience was held on January 7, 2007. That Sunday was a crazy day in a wonderful way! We simply did not know what to expect. Though we had planned for months, we were not sure what was going to happen. Everyone on our team was excited the morning of our launch. Olu called me at 5:30 a.m. We were laughing and joking when I asked, "Do you have your robe?" This was a joke because we don't wear robes. We wear blue jeans and t-shirts — we keep it casual.

When we arrived at the worship location, we were in for a surprise. None of us had listened to the weather report; so we didn't know it was supposed to rain on our opening day. Imagine planting a church, setting up, doing all the pre-work required, then waking up on the big day and it looks like rain. This may sound crazy but during all of our pre-launch preparations, we never really thought about the weather or what to do if conditions were inclement.

I didn't wake up thinking, "Okay; let me check the weather forecast." After seeing the signs of impending showers, I said to the team, "Alright, this is the day! It's time to go — let's get up and let's do it!" This same disregard for the small things (like the weather) was with us throughout our preparation to plant. We said, "Okay God, you called us to do this. You have given the vision, so we're going to do it and we're going to leave the rest up to You."

During the walk-through on Saturday, we felt a buzz in the air…that feeling of anticipation when you are about to go from concept to reality. You know it is reality when you move from paper to action. When we arrived at the worship site, we were thoroughly focused. The team was running around excited and doing last minute preparations. We were putting down wires and tape, trying to figure out if we had enough people to park the cars, double-checking the worship flow and other items on the to-do list. The joy of the Lord was our strength.

Despite the weather, people poured into the worship space. I remember standing backstage with Olu, who asked, "Do you see them? How many people are out there?" I said, "I don't want to know," but I looked from back stage and saw people waiting for worship to start. It felt like a grand opening of a movie. It was exciting to see the people arriving. I remember saying, "God, you're for real. You're awesome because I don't know if I'd have come out for a new church starting its first worship experience on a rainy Sunday."

The excitement in the air is what I remember most. The lights were dim. The smog machine was doing its thing and we sang, "Let's Get It Started" by the Black Eyed Peas. I had the awesome responsibility of opening up the worship experience. I went on stage, jumped up and down and screamed, "It's time! It's what you've been waiting for! It's a great day…you're making history today!"

The momentum was set and it lasted throughout the uniquely-ordained experience. No, inclement weather could not and did not stop the move of God at Impact on January 7, 2007!

MAKE AN IMPACT!

Do you remember the last time you stepped off the edge for God? How did it feel? Who was there? What did you see?

Why We Don't Have "Services"

We try not to call our worship time a "service" or a "Sunday morning worship service." An Impact experience begins in the parking lot; goes from the first words of praise to the last amen; and lingers long after people leave our presence. Every moment matters. What does the weekend experience look/feel like for you, your teams, your people, and your guests?

Be Present, Not Perfect

Olu and Edwin

More than 500 people attended our first day of worship. Pastors and planters are always concerned about having everything in place or having the highest number of people in worship that one can possibly gather. You want to make sure the children's piece is in place. You want to make sure the cookies are positioned correctly. You want to make sure the audio is right. We only wish all of those items had been in place on opening day. Everything was not in place and now five years later we are still tweaking and adjusting. We have come to realize ultimate perfection is something that takes place only in Heaven.

We host live worship experiences. Live means you don't get an opportunity to edit out technical glitches or human missteps. If the speaker system makes odd or unusual sounds, you have to deal with it. In the beginning, that was a hard reality for us because we spent so much time preparing and using every possible resource available to create a perfect experience.

We have learned that even when we plan the "perfect experience," it may not flow as we hoped. The blessing is to be at peace in the moment of worship. Just being a fully engaged participant in worship, knowing who you are in God is the greatest blessing. Even so, it is helpful to recognize that things are going to happen.

Our plan was to allow ample time for set up and to do a final tech check before the beginning of worship. We tried to be at the site by 8:00 a.m. for a 10:00 a.m. worship experience.

Even though we planned to run everyone through a sound check, some participants did not get one. Our creative director was concerned about this. I told the team we had to keep going. I said, "People are going to arrive at 10:00 a.m. and we have to stay committed to starting on time no matter what happens."

We didn't care if we had 6 people or if we had 600 people or if we had 2 lights or 2 microphones — we were going to start on time. The speaker system made a weird noise, and everybody jumped. The smoke machine had a mind of its own. And there were a couple other technical difficulties, but because we started on time, I feel everything worked out in the end.

 MAKE AN IMPACT!

What can you do to focus on the essence and blessing of an event and not become bogged down or disappointed with the mishaps?

Continual Improvement

Consider this: We want the worship experience to always evolve. To achieve this goal, we look at every experience objectively and evaluate its effectiveness. Each week, we search for ways to improve every aspect of worship experience at Impact.

Impact Idea 51 Creative Worship is a Multisensory Experience

Anja

Our Creative Worship team seeks to create a worship experience where people can honor and adore God in new, different and unique ways. One way to approach worship themes creatively is to approach them through more than one sense. Since God is in everything, God comes to us through a variety of senses.

Worship is more than the sermon. It is more than the music. It is more than the order of worship. Worship encompasses everything guests, participants see, taste, hear, smell and feel in the worship experience. One Sunday we were teaching about how the body is God's temple and the importance of worshipping God with our bodies. As a part of that worship experience, we invited a fitness instructor and a yoga instructor to help illustrate the message. The two instructors led simple exercises during the worship experience as examples of what we can do to help us maintain a healthy mind and body. The congregation followed their lead and really got into the exercises. People were out of their seats moving around the room. The experience was totally unexpected, unique and essential to bringing the teaching points to life for the congregation.

The entire leadership team stood in the back of the worship space amazed that people were actually doing what the instructors were leading them to do. Some people were in suits; others had on sweats; some had on shorts. It was a visible sign of people becoming involved in the worship experience. We worshipped God creatively, physically and spiritually that Sunday! During our worship experiences, we seek to maintain an atmosphere of surprise as we facilitate having an encounter with God. We rely on our creative teams to help us brainstorm possibilities. Then we make sure to mix it up from Sunday to Sunday.

MAKE AN IMPACT!

Begin using the senses (see, touch, taste, smell, and hear) to help incorporate creative elements in worship. Remember to mix it up to keep it creative and unpredictable.

Make Worship Unique, Not Uncomfortable

Anja and Olu

Our goal is to have a unique worship experience each week. People who are coming to Impact know they are going to experience something different when they arrive each Sunday. They come to worship expecting to feel the presence of God differently than they did last week.

For us, the importance of doing worship differently ties back into our brand — doing church differently. Promoting a different brand and keeping things fresh in worship are significant components of our success.

Many church leaders download service templates from denominational liturgy books. Others go to the internet to access the ABC's of a worship service document. These approaches may or may not offer a unique worship experience that speaks to your target mission field.

At Impact, we rethink worship from the ground up. We do this (as we do many things) with an eye toward attracting people who may not regularly attend church and people from mainstream culture with diverse interests and from diverse generational or cultural backgrounds. Our Creative Programming and Worship Teams help us cast our net wide.

In worship, we seek to make people comfortable and to break down barriers that prevent them from coming back to church. Part of how we do that is to incorporate things that are familiar to them. For example, we often use non-offensive secular music with a message or something that people can connect with. Using secular music to convey a message for

God may seem strange to some people. We know we are not only doing something different, but we are also connecting with them through something they like or something that applies to daily living.

When we use elements that they can relate to, worshippers are more comfortable. Guests feel as if we have something in common with them, as opposed to being holier or irrelevant to them. We seek to connect with people and create experiences where they are comfortable. If people are satisfied, they may just hang out long enough to explore and develop their own relationship with Christ.

 **MAKE AN IMPACT!**

What can you do to ensure each worship service has at least one element that is familiar to your mission field?

Worship that Lives and Breathes

We are an organic organization. We are an organization that lives and breathes. We are always striving to be fluid in all that we do. We have that same type of commitment to the worship experience. We want the worship experience to breathe, to grow and to live. Thus, we make a conscious and intentional decision NOT to do the same things from Sunday to Sunday.

Worship Planning is a Team Sport

53 *Olu & Anja*

Impact Idea

Olu's Perspective

Our worship planning and implementation represent a team led effort. While many pastors may think it sounds great, the ability to let go of ego and control is necessary. In many places, it is typical practice for pastors to lay out the whole worship service and then preach the sermon while keeping their eyes on the worship flow.

I participate in our worship experience planning process from a macro level. For Impact, that means helping to set overall themes for the next five or six months. With clear direction, I can shift my focal point to writing sermons. I begin working individually on the weekly sermons while the Creative Programming team develops the overall whole weekend worship experience.

In some instances, the work of the team may alter what I'm going to preach or the direction of preaching. I have discovered that the more input and advice I get, the better the sermon is; the more ideas I get about a whole worship theme or the total worship experience, the better the entire process is. Pastors who are looking for ways to improve worship should give it over to a team or trusted group of people. Developing plans in silos is not always the best approach.

Anja's Perspective

Our Creative Programming team is made up of four sub-teams:

- Administrative Team: Helps coordinate the behind-the-scenes technical and production agenda.
- Creative Expressions Team: Helps coordinate any creative worship expressions during a worship experience, i.e. dance, spoken word, music, drama, etc.
- Service Production Team: Serves as directors or producers during a live worship experience.
- Video Production Team: Documents the worship experience through videography and provides special video as needed to support the message.

While there are many ways to divide the planning and labor for creative worship, this method helps us to streamline decision-making and allows people to retain appropriate authority within their areas.

 **MAKE AN IMPACT!**

Describe your worship team. Does it help focus people and creativity in the right places? Is there little wasted time or energy? What next steps do you need to make in order to improve your team?

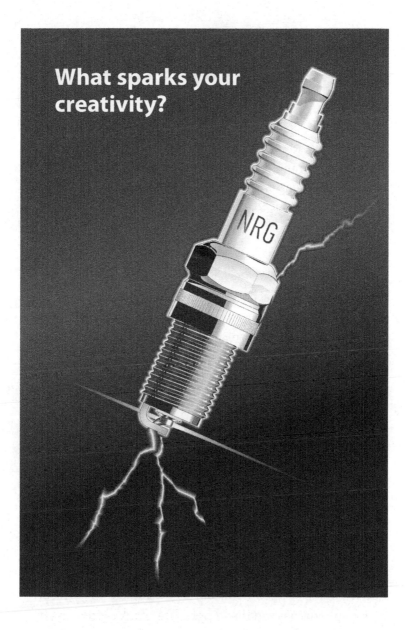

Impact Idea 54

God-Centered Creativity is Essential

Anja

We use an intentional, God-centered approach to planning worship. A month or so before we introduce a new sermon series, our Creative Programming team gathers to generate creative ideas for the topic based upon an outline given by our lead pastor.

The first thing we do is open ourselves up to God and to the word of God. We pray and ask God to open us up to be used creatively. Each person on the team is valued and is encouraged to bring forth a variety of unique ideas, each of us creating in our own way. This makes for a rich discussion because we all come to the "brainstorming table" with different experiences and perspectives. Using creative brainstorming techniques, we build on each other's ideas without regard for how "crazy" or doable the ideas may be. As John Maxwell, author of Thinking for a Change, explains, "Creative people are 'other' thinkers. They are always thinking about and looking for other ways of doing things because they know that options bring opportunities."[12]

Here is a glimpse of what the process felt like for one of my favorite four-week series: "Your Season Premiere." The series was about introducing the real you. At times, we may not live our lives as authentically as we could. "Your Season Premiere" emphasized the importance of taking the time to look at who you are; being real about who God has called you to be; and then being comfortable with introducing that person to the world.

The creative session for "Your Season Premiere" began in prayer, the same as all of our creative sessions. I introduced the premise of the series and we read through the scriptures associated with it. Then we started throwing out ideas and feeding off of one another:

"Ooo, let's bring in a tuba player!"
"Let's bring in a tuba player that is dressed up like a mascot."
"Interesting. Can the tuba player play something
that tubas shouldn't play?"

The point of initial brainstorming isn't to finalize everything but to exhaust the options. Sometimes we'll think through an idea for awhile and decide not to implement it. One of the ideas that we didn't embrace in the "Your Season Premiere" series involved mirrors. The idea was to use mirrors to remind people to examine themselves to see who they really are. We thought about how we could encourage people to actually look at themselves in the mirror throughout the worship experience. We decided not to use mirrors as part of the experience even though it was a great idea.

One of the things we implemented for this series was the use of promotional teaser spots similar to what you would see for a Hollywood film premier. Using these spots provided a way to generate interest in the series while communicating how important it is for each of us to take the huge step toward authentic living.

God is at the heart of our creative process. The journey involves discovering fresh ways to bring the Word to life and being in a loving and supportive community with one another to make a difference for those who come to worship with us each week.

 **MAKE AN IMPACT!**

Describe your creative worship planning process. Does it help focus people and creativity in the right places? Is there little wasted time or energy? What next steps do you need to take in order to improve your planning process?

Turn Creative Ideas into Executable Worship Activities

Anja

Our creative sessions tend to run between one to two hours and deal with two different tasks: idea generation and executable worship activities. Talking with each other about different ideas is the fun part. Translating those ideas into executable worship activities is the difficult task.

For each idea that we think is a "keeper," we work out how and whether or not to use it. We can't always do everything. With the list of ideas in mind, we have to evaluate what activities and resources we can actually accomplish. We ask:

- How much money will it cost? How does that compare with how much we have to work with?
- What props/resources do we already have that can be repurposed?
- What relationships do we have that may be leveraged to accomplish the idea?

Some research may be necessary if we decide to give away something or if we're going to invite a guest. All of that takes time. Phone calls have to be made; emails have to be sent. Additional meetings must be scheduled if we want to create a skit or a video piece. So many pieces go into translating an idea into an executable activity.

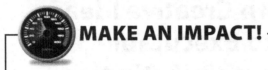 **MAKE AN IMPACT!**

Which of the following are getting in the way of implementing your creative ideas:

- Dismissing the idea as unaffordable

- Lack of research follow-through

- Reluctance to ask those outside the team — or even the church — for help

- Too few ideas from which to choose

- Lack of clarity about what might work in your worship flow

- Other (name what it is for you)

Using this, or a similar assessment, commit to address your major limitation this week.

Impact Idea 56

Excellent Worship Requires Daily Attention

Anja

Monday: Take it easy. At a maximum, I follow up on items that are significant and can't wait until Tuesday.

Tuesday: Meet with leaders. I spend about 30 minutes on the phone with each of the Creative Programming sub-team leads (administration team, creative expressions team, service production team, and video production team). We discuss what we need to do for the week, or look at what we did last week. In order for those phone conversations to be productive, I prepare well for them. I jot down specific ideas to discuss, what's coming down the pike, thoughts about Sunday, etc.

Wednesday: Create the "concept document" for Sunday's worship experience. The concept document basically takes all of the ideas and summarizes them in a form so that anybody participating in the worship experience has an understanding of what the day is going to be about. This document is used for Thursday's call.

Thursday: Solidify details for Sunday's worship experience. We conference call to review the concept document in order to solidify the ideas, make sure everything is in place and identify specific roles and responsibilities. At the end of the call, we will also begin talking about the next week or the next two or three themes. We check the concept document against what is in the Planning

Center[13] and make sure all of the details for Sunday are included. If they're not, we follow up until all details are complete (e.g., that we know what music the praise and worship team will sing, that we have details on any special guests who may be attending, that transitions that have to occur between one component of the service and the next are understood or spelled out.)

Friday: Advanced planning for the following week. By Friday we are set for Sunday; therefore, we can move ahead to the next Sunday worship experience. Do we have everything that we need? Did we pick up, or are we planning to pick up, any props? Do we have a final rehearsal scheduled? If not, do we have a ready and executable skit or video, or whatever it is we're planning for the experience?

Saturday: Final preparations for Sunday. This could include picking up and delivering props and attending to any other task that can be done prior to Sunday.

Sunday: Producers are responsible for helping the team of worship leaders implement the plan as designed. (See next Impact Idea.) After the worship experiences end, sometimes we will give emphasis to the current stage setup or examine possibilities for upcoming worship experiences. We may need to meet as a team to discuss a skit or a rehearsal of some sort.

MAKE AN IMPACT!

If you are like many people, this daily digest could have given you a headache. Find the person who gets excited by this list and you just may have found a perfect team leader.

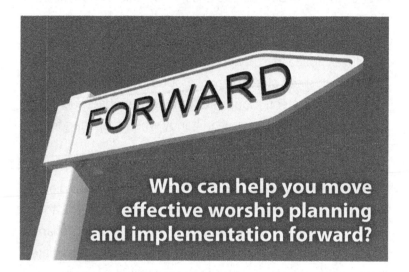

FORWARD

Who can help you move effective worship planning and implementation forward?

Partner with God to Produce the Worship Experience

Impact Idea 57

Anja and Olu

Worship is a live experience: a dynamic, ever-flowing, ever-changing experience. To ensure a seamless and efficient flow, we have employed several practices from the radio and television world. Specifically, we have a "tech sheet" and a "producer" for each experience.

The tech sheet gives the background detail of the various worship components along with time, leader notes and other information that might come in handy when preparing for or troubleshooting live worship.

The producer arrives no later than 8:30 Sunday morning or even earlier when something exceptionally complex is happening. Our worship experiences are at 10:00 a.m. and 12:00 noon. The producer comes with the tech sheet in hand (printout of the flow of the day, our checklist) and immediately starts setting-up props where they are needed, and making sure the stage is in good shape. As the musicians warm up, the producer facilitates getting a quality sound check. Finally, the producer reviews the tech sheet with all worship leaders to ensure everyone has a clear understanding of their role in the worship experience for the day. The producer highlights anything special they need to do (e.g., hand off a microphone, exit the stage in a different direction, etc.) The producer makes sure the lighting is set up appropriately and asks if there are any questions about cues or transitions. The producer knows what the entire experience should be and is there to help facilitate the plan. When we recruit producers, we look for people who are cool and calm under pressure; people who have a heart for worship, and who are able to multi-task all the details and components that go into our worship experiences. Producers also need input, respect and support from the leaders involved in the worship experience.

All worship leaders understand that God is the ultimate designer and developer of every worship experience. Producers stand ready to cue and troubleshoot as needed.

MAKE AN IMPACT!

How do you partner with God in worship? As you consider your unique environment, would the concept of a "tech sheet" and/or "producer" be useful?

Impact Idea 58
Look to Culture for Creative Worship Sparks

Anja

Creativity is endless and infinite. It is the very heart of God. We've done many different things with the intent of encouraging people to experience God and we've only scratched the surface as it relates to creativity. We want to use more sound effects and more creative lighting. Our aim is to awaken and touch all of the senses and help people experience God through each one of them (Impact Idea #51).

We seek to:

- Use different art forms. We use a lot of contemporary secular music. We have used spoken word. One Sunday, we had nothing but spoken word artists deliver the message. That was a unique experience.
- Use comedy. There are many talented Christian comedians that can help deliver a message from God through comedy. You may even have some stand-up comics in your circle of relationships.
- Use local or national events. We had an awesome worship experience one Super Bowl Sunday. We were able to use the Super Bowl as a springboard to develop a creative worship experience that used a popular event as a connection to spiritual development.
- Be inspired by our stories and the stories of others as springboards into new examples, new metaphors and new ideas.

MAKE AN IMPACT!

Where do you look for creative sparks?

Impact Idea 59

Creativity Can Come in Small Packages

Anja

You may be wondering about the small steps you can take to make your worship services more creative.

With any change, you want to start small.

Probably the simplest thing to do is to use props in your worship experience. Explore the use of metaphor as the lesson of the day is unfolding. The metaphor could come directly from the scripture, from what it evokes or the theme of the day. For example, the words in Isaiah 64:8:

> *Yet, O LORD, you are our Father.*
> *We are the clay, you are the potter;*
> *we are all the work of your hand.*

You could simply use Play-Doh to illustrate the point. For a more complex experience, give everyone in the congregation a piece of Play-Doh, or have a potter with a wheel come and demonstrate the various stages in throwing, firing and recycling pots to illustrate God's relationships to us.

Illustrate your point with a popular secular song. You can say it, sing it, play a recording of it or have your band or choir prep it. Just be sure to include songs from a variety of generations so everyone can get in on the fun or pun!

You can simply take something out of your worship experience that you're currently doing and substitute it with a different way of doing it. For example, instead of doing a standard altar call for individuals to kneel and pray, use that time differently. Give everyone a piece of stationery and a pencil. While the music plays, have each person write a love letter to God.

Start small. See how people respond and what resonates. Soon you will find your own unique ways of making powerful changes in your worship experience.

 **MAKE AN IMPACT!**

If you are worshiping already, implement one small creative idea next Sunday. Don't be afraid to try something different.

Logistics

DRIVE TO STAY ON TASK, ON POINT, AND ON TIME

Double Your Capacity with a Logistics Coordinator

Impact Idea 60

Olu and Maxine

Logistics and planning are essential to the effectiveness of a new or existing church. In October of our first year, we realized we needed to launch a second worship experience and Edwin and I knew we could not launch it by ourselves. We needed somebody who had administrative and logistics capability to give oversight to the whole area and let us know what needed to be done and when it needed to be done. We needed someone with the ability to communicate with every team leader to ensure all were on the same page. When we launched our first worship experience in January 2007, we didn't have a Coordinator. Consequently, we found ourselves trying to manage many variables outside our gift mix.

You may be wondering what a Logistics Coordinator does. Maxine (Max) Fears (Impact's first salaried Logistics Coordinator) shares her understanding of the role:

In short, I do detail. What I've discovered is a lot of times the world seems divided into two types of people. You have one person who's the visionary — that person sees the big ideas. And then you have the nuts and bolts person. The two go together on any team. Often the big picture person has a problem reaching closure because it's a step-by-step process. The nuts and bolts person enjoys the details.

When Max began to manage logistics, she doubled our capacity. Originally she came on board as coordinator for our second worship experience launch. We realized we could not function without her; therefore, we created a position for her called "Logistics Coordinator." Now, she uses her skills and talent across the entire organization. Immediately, I moved all logistics-related activities from my portfolio to hers. The first responsibility I gave to Max was communication with teams. In church planting and general organizational growth, you can quickly reach your individual and personal limits. This can be a good thing if properly handled and others are allowed to lead. In this case, I knew if we didn't have a volunteer or paid staff person focused on our logistics, the whole organization would suffer. That didn't mean that I stopped interfacing with the teams altogether, but team leaders knew that they eventually were going to have to talk with Max about anything related to logistics.

As the leader at Impact, I realized I couldn't do it all and shouldn't try to do it all. Moreover, I needed to maximize my time to successfully execute my responsibilities relative to vision casting and the other day-to-day activities.

MAKE AN IMPACT!

This would be a great opportunity for you to write down the names and roles of each person on your lead team. Ask the following questions:

What are our logistics gaps? Who is gifted in logistics? Where do we need to place extra logistics support?

Ideal Logistics Person Profile

Look for a person who has a passion for three things: details, communication, and people. Those are the three ingredients. Your logistics coordinator has to be the type of person who can plan, who can look at the overall picture, and at the same time, see the nuts and bolts. The coordinator also has to be a communicator. To be successful your logistics coordinator must know how to listen to people and how to respond to their ideas.

Keep an Eye on Impact of Great Ideas

Maxine

The logistics process starts when someone gives you an idea and asks you to make it happen. Once I've been given the idea I have to understand it and then think about the details and timeline. Here are the questions I need answered:

1. What is the expected outcome? I need to know what the idea is about, what it seeks to accomplish. I need to see the vision and buy into it.
2. Can we get from A to Z in time? Is the timeframe workable? Can we make this happen on Sunday even though the update came on Friday, or should we wait until next week or next month?
3. Does the idea's topic conflict with other items on the timeline? Will it send a mixed message?
4. Who's involved? Who else needs to be aware of the idea or event? Who do I need to communicate with?

A part of the logistics coordinator's job is to assess the cost functionality (time, energy, money, people, clarity) of each idea and the idea mix. We're a new church and we have lots of great ideas. Additionally, we're really growing and we have created an environment of shared leadership. Two or three teams may come up with different ideas to be handled on the same Sunday or week. A part of the logistics coordinator's job is to make sure the ideas are doable and don't conflict.

For example, one Sunday we wanted to serve a big cake to celebrate another milestone: over 1,000 in attendance. Fortunately, I became aware that another group was planning a diabetes awareness campaign on the same day. When I reviewed my notes, I realized that having a cake on diabetes awareness Sunday was not going to flow. Of course, we rescheduled the celebration with cake on another Sunday and all went well.

If we had allowed both to occur on the same Sunday, we would have sent a mixed message and people would have been confused that particular Sunday. It is really important for the logistics coordinator to keep an eye on the overall impression made by the implementation of great ideas. Sometimes the church planter or organizational leader doesn't see the big picture from as many angles as they might like. The logistics person provides an essential viewpoint that helps the organization stay on task and on message.

If you don't remember anything else, remember this: use every opportunity to plant the right seeds. Communication and planning and a dependable logistics coordinator can make sure your intentions and messages are clear the first time.

 **MAKE AN IMPACT!**

What is your process for helping your congregation stay on time, on track and on message? Who is responsible for this process and its outcomes?

Are Your Ideas In Sync?

Impact Idea 62
Approach Ministry Like an Event or Meeting Planner

Maxine

My passion is meeting planning. Through several experiences, I discovered that organizing is my gift. What is more, it is a transferable skill that can be used in the corporate world as well as in a church environment.

The launch of our second worship experience provides a good example. As we discussed before, the first step is to identify the outcome. The expected outcomes of the second experience launch were to:

- have the same energy/quality as the opening service, and
- ensure the combined attendance at the current 10:00 a.m. worship experience and the newly- launched noon experience total 1,000 people or more.

As we prepared for launch, I identified the people and teams that needed to be included by considering who was going to be involved, who needed to plan, and who was going to be "touched" by the plan.

Once you have established the what (outcome) and who (people and teams, audience) is involved, then you can focus on communicating the vision and the plan. Make sure everybody is on the same page. Be sure you listen to their concerns and address them so that everybody may be brought into the conversation.

Use the feedback to design and develop the plan. Once the outcome is shared and concerns are expressed and discussed, develop a step-by-step plan that specifies who is involved, the tasks they are doing, and the timeline for completing those tasks. What does this team need to know? What does this team already know? If two teams are involved, how do they interact? (See Appendix B: 2nd Launch Plan.)

Once the plan is developed, I serve as a hands-on project manager and communicator until the event (in this case worship launch) is implemented. I make sure that everybody understands what is happening on a daily basis and what their part is in making it happen. Monitoring progress is really important, especially once you "go live."

When the big day arrives, the planner's job is to review the implementation and make changes as needed. After the event is over, a post-evaluation is critical:

1. Celebrate the people. Never start out saying, "This is what went wrong." We did the event; now we need to celebrate it.

2. Encourage everybody to take a look at how to make it better the next time. Help people understand that the process can always be improved.

MAKE AN IMPACT!

Choose a large event that is being planned or is on the near horizon. Using the ideas above, work the process:

1. Choose an Event or Ministry
2. Identify the Outcome
3. Identify Teams and People Impacted
4. Communicate Vision
5. Create a Plan
6. Manage the Project
7. Execute the Project
8. Celebrate
9. Evaluate
10. Improve

Impact Idea 63

Facilitated Planning is One Way God Makes a Way

Edwin and Maxine

In church culture, we don't always do what we need to do, because it's easier to say, "God will work it out" or "The Lord will make a way."

At the end of the day, if we're going to be serious about reaching people from all spectrums of culture, who work and live in places where things have to be on the up-and-up, we have to meet these expectations. We don't want anyone to come into our environments and find us lagging behind. We don't want anyone to come to a mission project and discover that nobody knows what's going on. We don't want anyone coming to a special event that was supposed to start at 7:00, but then starts at 7:30.

We need to take pre-planning, execution and post-evaluation very seriously because nobody wants to come to an event that's chaotic, where people obviously don't know what they are doing. Volunteers don't want to show up to help and realize no one knows what they are expected to do. Christian facilitators and planners must understand that God moves through the planning process:

As Max, our Logistics Coordinator says:

"I believe that God always makes a way, and most of the time God's way involves working through people. I think of it this way — God gave me a gift to plan, to help people get from a to z. I'm a part of how God is making a way.

I'm a part of making the way as a planner, project manager, and facilitator. Facilitating groups through the steps of the planning process is something that helps continue to grow and evolve leaders, while simultaneously creating excellence.

Imagine being in your church with your leaders and in 90 minutes everybody walks out having felt heard and having a clear understanding about next steps. That is God making a way through facilitated planning.

MAKE AN IMPACT!

Identify the potential human resources that God has provided to help with planning, project management, logistics and/or facilitation. Take them to lunch or for coffee and find out where God may be seeking to use them to make a way in your setting.

Include Logistics of Volunteers

Maxine and Edwin

The logistics position evolved for us. I can remember standing in the back of the auditorium during one worship experience observing a significant number of people who, it seemed, did not know who could help them with general support or assistance. I remember that Olu looked at me and said, "We've got to find somebody who can point our volunteers and attendees in the direction they need to go."

This was the first project we identified as a need. Since then, many more projects have evolved.

Some are ongoing projects like team assessment (see Impact Idea 65). Other projects meet a short-term need. As we grow, additional changes and systems develop on our horizon. Some of these changes involve combining teams or dividing teams. Some of the teams I work with to redefine roles and reposition leaders and/or processes.

Currently we are actively working to increase our volunteer base. As we grow, we need more volunteers. This project entails everything from researching online recruitment tools to training and ensuring that each team becomes responsible for training and maintaining their own volunteers.

In addition, there are external logistics needs. We receive many support requests from the broader community. We have to process the requests in a timely fashion. Our desire is to have a positive impact on our community at large, but that becomes a little difficult when there are only a certain number of hours in a day. Processing these requests has become a logistics project because Max consults with the person making the request to assess what, exactly, he or she needs from Impact.

MAKE AN IMPACT!

What logistics projects do you currently have in your portfolio? What do you need to transition out of your portfolio? What do you need to add to your portfolio?

Impact Idea 65

Create Volunteer Empowerment Systems

Edwin and Maxine

We expose our staff and volunteers to a variety of leadership activities. After these experiences, we meet together and unpack the learning. It is important that we create a space for our teams and our leaders where they are able to process their experiences:

- "Okay, this is what I have."
- "You know what, this is what I don't like; this is what I like."
- "I am going to apply this to my particular area of ministry."
- Our logistics coordinator does a lot of work relating to all of our team leaders. For us, that's big. It helps us to set up clear, effective and efficient systems.

Sometimes people think when we say "doing church differently," it means we have no plan. Different means we are going to do something different; something we may not associate with church. It doesn't mean we don't have a plan. Max works with each of our teams to create their own procedures and systems:

We establish procedures with each team. We empower each team to own their responsibility: to define it, to manage it. One of the most important things about developing systems is the understanding that the systems work only if the people who are supposed to follow them understand them and buy in. If they don't understand and buy in, the systems don't work. One example of "doing it differently" is the degree to which we are open. We listen to what our team members have to say and customize the process so that the process reflects their ideas.

I serve as a guide, sounding board, and source of encouragement for staff and volunteers. The person who says, make sure you're communicating. Make sure you've thought through the process. Our teams are the ones who are coming up with the ideas and I'm providing guidance to make sure they can carry those ideas from zero to eighty.

Periodically we've had to evaluate different team areas and team leaders to ensure that we've got the right people doing the right things.

I approach this process the same way I would approach any event or project planning. First I ask about the purpose of the team. What does the team do? Once we define what the team does, and what the process should be for that particular team, I talk to the team leaders. I find out what their skills are. Where they are gifted? Then I make sure that those skills and gifts are a fit with the team. If they are a fit, I talk with the team leaders to make sure they're getting the training, the feedback and the empowerment that they need to move forward in bolder, mightier ways.

Like everything here, the leader empowerment system is an ongoing evaluation and improvement process. Nothing is ever stagnant at Impact.

 **MAKE AN IMPACT!**

Choose your most essential team. Using the ideas above, evaluate and improve that team.

Take Baby Steps

Maxine

First of all, take a look at your church, your organization, and ask, "Where do we want to go? What do we want to accomplish? And what do I want to do?" Taking baby steps means first writing down the things that you want to accomplish; then, determining the simple, strategic steps needed to get you there. Include the people, the tasks and the timing. Baby steps involve constantly evaluating where you are and where you want to go. Then you start a step-by-step planning process. A lot of information is available, but nothing beats deciding where you want to be and then planning for it.

Taking baby steps means assessing one ministry at a time or one team at a time instead of trying to evaluate them all at once. It means planning then doing, one step at a time. A starting point could be training or having a strategy session or simply observing and asking questions. No one can actually tell you how to change your organization. The only thing someone can tell you is that planning is critical and that you must start planning.

Initially, I worked diligently with the Hospitality Team. I started there because hospitality is our first point of contact. I had to take time to understand the purpose of the hospitality team. I listened to members of the team explain their purpose. I shadowed them one Sunday. Then I had to think about what our guests experience when they come into the Impact environment.

Based on my observations and conversations, we established orientation guidelines. We talked about extreme customer service. From the minute someone enters an Impact environment, we are eager to know what that person expects to experience. That's extreme customer service.

Our team leaders are empowered with the idea of extreme customer service. Now they train their own volunteers. They know how to bring the volunteers in, how to schedule volunteers, and how to improve constantly, as well as how to redefine the level of customer service.

Plan to succeed. Build your organization and grow your church by taking one step at a time.

 **MAKE AN IMPACT!**

Select one team that is the most important to improve. Identify what they need/want to accomplish and plan baby steps to get them there.

Staffing

DRIVE TOWARD A STAFF-LED, RIGHT FIT MODEL

Invest in Human Resources

Dawn and Olu

A year and one month into the launch of Impact, we had 19 staff persons: two of them full-time, 17 part-time. We endured some growing pains before we realized the benefits of hiring a Human Resources specialist. Bringing people onboard would have been a whole lot easier. New hires could have gone through an orientation and training process to ensure they truly understood and lived out the DNA and vision of Impact. Though we changed our strategy late in the game, we had the good sense to bring Dawn Wright on as an HR specialist during our second year.

One of the most important assets Impact has is people: our human capital/resources. It is critical that we have the right fit in the right place in the right position so that Impact can continue to push the envelope while staying on track with its vision and DNA. We seek to find that right fit for everyone involved — not just for Impact, but for the person being hired as well.

The commitment to secure the right people is a recurring theme in Jim Collins' book, *Good to Great*.[14] When we find good fits, everyone benefits. Impact is growing, and staff stay engaged as they serve and grow according to what they are called and hired to do.

In the church planting world, they say we live or die based on the number of people who attend our experiences. We understand that the way we treat people is directly related to those numbers. We have to bring leaders onboard who are relationally aware — people who will treat people right — in addition to being technically proficient. We need to employ people who feel motivated to invest their talent and energy into making the vision a reality.

Impact is a place that doesn't settle for the status quo. To thrive at Impact, staff must enjoy rocking the boat and trying new things. We're constantly "testing the waters." We don't mind being trailblazers. We don't mind saying, "Just because it's never been done before doesn't mean we're never going to try to do it."

Our HR specialist is so important to the alignment and momentum of the ministry and to protecting the vision, that we wish we had started out of the box with the position. Dawn serves as a recruiter and gatekeeper. She articulates and lives out our vision as it relates to finding people. She provides an orientation and an ongoing feedback process for the right people who want to come in and be a part of what we do.

"The right staff members are an investment rather than an expense."[15]

 **MAKE AN IMPACT!**

Who serves as your recruiter and gatekeeper? Does that person have the right skills and gifts to do the job in a way that creates alignment and momentum for ministry and organizational growth?

Impact Idea 68

Consider Moving to a Staff-Led Model

Dawn and Edwin

From our inception we knew we wanted to be staff-led. Being staff-led doesn't mean we don't employ volunteers heavily…we do. Before we started we believed putting staff in key leadership roles would help us accelerate our impact. With this model, we're using an entire staff of people: technical, music, creative director, finance, etc. We seek to have a staff person in every area essential for running a business.

Being staff-led is a risk, but there are definite benefits. The benefits of a staff-led model include being able to attract personnel with particular skill sets, with clearer accountability and increased coordination. It is definitely something that pushes the envelope within church culture for two reasons:

- we spend more money on staff than a typical new church start or even most existing churches, and
- we trust a smaller group of people to lead in alignment with the vision/purpose/mission of the organization.

In a new church start, the only person typically receiving any compensation is the pastor, maybe a part-time administrator and/or maybe a music director or worship leader. This hiring pattern maintains the pastor as the central authority. In our staff-led model, the role of the pastor(s) is decentralized. We are equipping people and giving them the authority to make the vision of Impact happen. To mitigate the risks inherent in this, we are constantly checking for vision commitment and alignment.

Go ahead and take the staff risk. You may already have a dynamic team, and perhaps the team is filled with volunteers. If you feel you need to go in a different direction, or to the next level, you may want to consider hiring staff. While you can go in a different direction or to the next level with volunteers, it helps to supplement with staff. Take the risk and we will see you in God's preferred future.

 **MAKE AN IMPACT!**

Identify 1–3 areas in your organization that are in constant need of improvement. Are any of these areas crying out for a qualified part-time or full-time staff person?

Hire for Present and Future Fit

Dawn and Olu

The purpose of hiring, moving, promoting and exiting staff is to grow and improve the organization. We seek to find, position and transition people so that Impact grows and improves. We look for high-capacity people — people who can come aboard and quickly understand our processes; people who have the skill set to take us to the next level. Let's say we are looking for candidates for an IT position. While we see from their resumes that they meet the skill set we are seeking today, we really want to know, "How can they help us in the future?" We look to see what they bring. At present, they may be performing above where we need them to be, in terms of scale, depth or breadth…but that isn't enough. They also need to have the ability to help us move to the next level on a consistent basis. They have to have the capacity, the knowledge, the ability and the skills to move us to level one, level two, level three, and level four.

We must put the right people in the right seats, people who can grow the organization in the right places. The process of determining who they are goes beyond gaining an understanding of their skills, abilities and previous experiences. We seek to determine: Do they fit where we're going? Do they fit what we're looking for? Are we a right fit for them? Can they come in and move like a streak of lightening for the organization? Can they challenge the organization in a healthy way?

One of the most important questions we ask is: *"What will you add to Impact? Or in other words, what will you bring to Impact that Impact does not already have?"* The way they answer that question is critical. Their answer reveals what they get and don't get about the Impact vision and operations and how they see themselves fitting into the organization.

More than one leader interviews prospective hires. The team leaders and members of the team also interview them. A right fit for everyone involved yields chemistry and longevity. It is important for the team members to have their say. Give them an early opportunity to ask questions and find out who is in it for the long haul. It is important that they stick with the organization during the good and not-so-good times that will come to pass in a growing a church.

MAKE AN IMPACT!

Are all of your leaders (paid and unpaid) growing their ministries in a way that grows the church and the kingdom of God? Remember always to ask: "What do you want to add to our church? What do you want to bring to us that we don't already have?"

Recruit Beyond Church Culture Alone

Dawn

Create a staffing plan and look at what it will take to bring that plan to fruition. Moving the model to reality involves clarifying what is needed, when it is needed, and how to pay for it. After those pieces are in place, it is time to recruit.

We encourage church leaders who are serious about reaching new people and growing their congregations to look beyond the typical places when hiring staff. If you're really serious about reaching a certain culture, then you need to employ people who are part of that culture.

Post jobs in traditional and non-traditional places: online, different schools in your area, and theatres. Talk to people one on one. Observe people and listen for their passion and experience on the street, on the subway, on the playground, at parties, in restaurants, etc. Strike up conversations in movie theaters and other arenas where people gather: Ask: "What do you do? What would you like to do?" Say: "I may have an opportunity for you."

Those are the avenues we use to identify potential Impact staff personnel. Once we find the right person, we typically negotiate the salary required to convince them to accept a position at Impact. The negotiation may involve a creative solution process. For example, we have had to adjust the numbers in the financial package in order to hire some people on our staff. Impact wants to hire and retain quality people, so we work to make sure they are being adequately compensated.

In some instances, we have full time-responsibilities for

potential staff, but only part-time funds. We find creative ways to honor the staff to ensure they feel valued, loved, and respected. Feeling a sense of success increases their sense of wellbeing and passion for what they're doing.

 **MAKE AN IMPACT!**

Where are you looking for people to hire? How is that connected to your process for recruiting the best and "right" talent?

Look for the 4 C's

Olu and Dawn

In his classic book, *Courageous Leadership*, Bill Hybels describes his hiring criteria: "The selection process for building Kingdom dream teams is based on "three Cs"..:"first character, then competence, and finally, chemistry... Character, Competence, Chemistry."[16] At Impact, we added a fourth C for Charisma.

Character is about personal integrity and includes determining whether prospective hires embody the values and culture of your church. Character is critical because they will represent your church or organization internally as well as in the community. The people you hire must have strong character.

Competency is about ensuring that the person has the applied knowledge and demonstrated ability to do tasks and carry out responsibilities required by the position. A resumé will give you a sense of the person's experience, but past performance indicates his or her level of competency.

Chemistry is what happens when one person's spark combines with the sparks of others on the team. Chemistry is about the synergy of how a person gels with the other people in the ministry. Do these sparks create a short-circuit or a bonfire? Chemistry is related to charisma.

Charisma is that spark in people that positively changes the atmosphere. They walk into a room and have an immediate impact. People are saying: "Oh, I have to find out what that person is doing." Charismatic people naturally attract and inspire others. We are looking for natural spiritual leaders who have charisma.

Underestimating the importance of any one of the four Cs will result in frustration and a need to take corrective action. Save yourself some time and headaches. Always evaluate the candidates' possibilities and responsibilities according to the four Cs!

MAKE AN IMPACT!

Think about the last hire (or assignment of a volunteer to a key leadership role) that didn't work. Which of the four C's was missing? How will you assess for that C in the future?

Impact Idea 72
Orient Early, Intentionally and Relationally

Dawn

It is helpful to have new hires meet everybody on the team as soon as possible. Bring them in; introduce them to the people who are involved in key decision-making roles and those who will work closely with them.

Impact is developing a four-week orientation for new hires. (Four weeks seems long, but Impact is a different type of organization.) During this orientation period, we envision having new staff work in every area of Impact so they can see the organization from every viewpoint. We don't need them to understand how to do the tasks outside their area, but we do need them to understand the hopes, challenges, relationships, decision-making and communication interface between their area and the rest of the organization. In doing so they gain an understanding of how the role they play is an important part in the context of all the other areas of Impact.

We also try to get them acclimated to what they will be doing from the very beginning, step by step by step. One of the trickier steps is bringing people on board in an area that was previously volunteer-led.

When a volunteer leader is replaced by paid staff, we are intentional about addressing the volunteer's unspoken questions: "What am I going to do now? They're hiring someone and they are paying them. Why haven't they been paying me?" To make the transition work best for everyone involved, we

All In

start by talking with the volunteer. We thank them for all that they've done to develop the area; explain what skill set was needed; explain how they can be used in the future (perhaps in that same area); and learn what the volunteer wants to do next. We then take the time to debrief the new staff person so that they understand how the volunteer feels.

Finally, from the very beginning, we establish the expectation of personal and professional growth with new staff. One way of doing this is through asking where they are growing next. We ask: What is one goal in your professional life you hope to achieve? How can Impact help you achieve your goal?

 MAKE AN IMPACT!

What is your process for training new leaders, paid and unpaid? What ideas would be useful to incorporate now?

Impact Idea 73

Understand What a Smart Internal Hire Looks Like

Dawn

Take a look at what your goals are, where you want to be in the future, and how you want to get there. When you are considering staffing, you are looking at an investment. Make sure that you're not afraid to take the leap. That leap is likely to involve concerns about your budget limitations. Can your organization afford the new position and the new hire? Bringing someone onboard may cost you $40,000 annually but it may help to think about it more incrementally (e.g., $3,333 per month, $770 per week or $110 per day) to help make sure you don't get cold feet.

When done right, internal hiring can be cost effective and can help you grow and protect your healthy DNA. A part of this equation involves identifying people who are in a season where they aren't looking for income as much as they are looking for fulfillment and/or flexibility. For example, look for a professional who has stepped off a fast track career in order to be more available to his/her family, or for someone who is considering early retirement. This is another reason why having relationships with people in your church or organization matters. You can't know where people are vocationally unless you know them personally. A part of knowing someone is learning about his/her goals and dreams. Sometimes relationships position us to learn about a change that might create a win-win situation. In other words, maybe somebody is retiring next week and is looking for something new in life that just so happens to match a hiring need of yours.

This leads to the strategic aspect of a smart, internal hire: look at your goals and identify the most important area for you to grow, with an eye toward the future.

1. What position will help you move from point A to point B?
2. Who can quickly step into the position that will take you from point A to point B? Look within your organization to see if there is someone who may be a best fit for you.
3. Before making an offer, closely examine the situation and job fit. Evaluate how the prospect can fulfill the hopes and dreams for the future in the proposed role.

Let the needs of the position — now and in the future — drive your understanding of who would be a good fit. Don't be afraid to keep your eyes and ears open for a great internal candidate!

MAKE AN IMPACT!

Define the first (or next) hire you need to make using the questions above to guide you. Look to your congregation or personal network and see if anyone emerges as a "fit." If not, consider posting the job externally. You may want to look internally and externally at the same time.

!mpact Idea 74 Give Everybody the Opportunity to Succeed

Edwin and Dawn

In order to succeed, leaders must be aligned with the vision. A leader who is not aligned with our vision cannot succeed at Impact.

We make sure the vision is in front. We communicate vision consistently and constantly. We make sure our leaders understand it. One of the ways we do this is by asking them two questions: "What is the vision of Impact?" and "What does the vision mean to you?" By interpreting the vision back to us, they give invaluable feedback about how they are or are not aligned. As visionary leaders, we must listen carefully to them and their interpretation of the vision.

We want everybody to have an opportunity to succeed. We increase the degree of success through training, seeking the right fit, and ensuring that everybody understands the vision. We put the vision in front of leaders daily, weekly, and monthly. We are constantly seeking to understand where our leaders are, both personally and professionally.

Impact staff members know that if they are having a difficult season, their Executive Team Leader or the HR Specialist will come to talk with them — not to transition them but to determine what the problem is. We encourage them to let us know what is getting in the way of performing up to par. If we intentionally build that kind of relationship with each leader, it helps us to create a very nurturing, yet accountable, space.

In that relational space, we discover whether or not they are continuing to grow or if it is time for a different opportunity. Again, building relationships is tied to success.

 **MAKE AN IMPACT!**

List the things you do to give everyone on your team the opportunity to succeed. Now add one more thing to that list and implement it this week.

Scheduled Maintenance

DRIVE TOWARD EFFECTIVENESS FOR THE LONG HAUL

Impact Idea 75
Do Not Allow Anyone to Compromise the Vision of the Organization

Dawn and Olu

Whether you are just starting to build your staff or you already have a staff in place, you will surely encounter staffing woes. When two, three, four, five or six people are in a room, you will certainly find multiple personalities, multiple styles, and multiple viewpoints that sometimes create friction. Some dissension is a necessary part of growth. Other conflict grows out of the fact that an individual is simply a bad match. Once we realize we have someone who is not the right fit, we have an obligation — for the sake of the vision — to transition that person to another area.

During the transition we operate from an understanding of vision, grace and the "bottom line." In the end, we cannot allow anyone to compromise the vision of the organization.

We all have different personalities, gifts and approaches. We seek to impress on leaders that we are all different and we must value our differences. We must not look at them as a negative, but as a positive; because everyone has something to bring to the table that can help grow the kingdom of God.

Balancing grace and the "bottom line" is really tough because transitioning leaders in and out of Impact is never easy. This is true for volunteers as well as paid staff. Each transition requires that we acknowledge and speak to the feelings involved. For instance, there are always strong feelings when a new staff hire is brought into an area that had been led by a volunteer — a volunteer who spent countless hours — hours that they could have spent elsewhere — leading a ministry. Naturally, feelings are aroused by the concept that "this was mine. Now it's being taken away from me." Some volunteers may even wonder, "Why didn't they hire me?" Still others feel like everything they did was pointless and/or unappreciated.

We work hard to let leaders who are being transitioned know they have done a great job. In the case of replacing a volunteer lead with a staff lead, we also make sure we have identified a new area that has the volunteer's name on it: a place that needs them, a place waiting for them to embrace and even to expand when it's time for them to move forward. We approach these transitions with love, appreciation, and with God's grace.

When we planted Impact, we realized that the vision of an organization is the foundation of its success. If the vision is ever compromised, danger lies ahead. The leaders of the organization are charged with the task of identifying the source of compromise. The issue has to be addressed by having a conversation with the responsible party. The purpose of the conversation is to discover if there are things that are distracting them from executing the vision, or if something has changed for them that alters how they view the vision. Once the conversation ends and the gaps are identified, partner with them to settle differences or bring about a solution. If this approach does not work, a transition may be needed.

 **MAKE AN IMPACT!**

Is there anyone in your organization who is compromising the vision? If so, schedule a conversation to see why. First, try to find a solution that will keep the person on the team. If this doesn't work, be open and honest with yourself about the possibility of transition.

Celebrate!

Olu and Edwin

The lowest number we have seen in weekend worship attendance has been in the three hundreds. In our first year, we were blessed to have five to six hundred people attend Impact regularly. Because things were growing exponentially, we launched a second worship time in October 2007.

When we added the second worship experience, attendance grew by 100–200 people. It was truly a blessing. On January 13, 2008, one year after Impact launched its first worship experience, something phenomenal happened. Over 1,000 people participated in Sunday worship. We remember the exact number: 1,136 people!

It was a mind-blowing experience. Later that day as we were talking about the worship event, we began to downplay the fact that there were 1,136 people worshipping with us. We weren't putting our stock in the number of people coming each week. In the past, whenever we had had a surprisingly high number of people in worship, we thanked God. We were grateful but we didn't make a big deal about it. When 1,136 people showed up for worship, we were thankful as usual, but we sensed we shouldn't move forward without a celebration.

A couple of weeks later we planned a major celebration in worship to emphasize the importance of naming and claiming our blessing. We ordered four large cakes with the inscription, "Over 1000." Everyone received a piece of cake, and we had a wonderful occasion of fellowship and reflection.

Little did we know that this event would set up the precedent for celebrations at Impact.

Celebrate!

What are you waiting for?

We place importance on celebration and we do take time to celebrate. In doing so, we value all of our staff and all of our teams and attendees. Our goal is to let people know they are unique and valued; so, we celebrate major accomplishments related to growth, numbers of people, types of experiences, and new ideas.

Celebrating is fun. We believe God has a very funny and creative side. This is why we believe there is real value in making the church experience pleasurable for those who are serving and for those who are coming, so that they can go out and share the fact that we can experience excitement in serving God. We hope you never forget the joyful side of ministry.

 **MAKE AN IMPACT!**

What do you do to celebrate the personal blessings God has given you? Take time to celebrate God's favor in your life. Take time to plan time and occasions to celebrate those who support the vision God has given you.

Impact Idea 77
Recalibrate to Serve Your Organization's Mission

Olu

Most church structures seem to encourage and increase focus on bureaucracy. Often it is difficult for these church organizations to stay focused on the "real thing" because their members and administrative teams are more caught up in the bureaucracy of the organization than the mission of the organization. If you spend more time in meetings than in doing ministry or in mission, you may need to recalibrate your structure. If you spend more total time attending leadership team meetings, reviewing procedures and budgets and updating one another about what has happened since the last meeting, you may need to recalibrate your structure.

Our churches and congregations must be mission-based and not maintenance-based. Unfortunately, many of our local churches are structured not to encourage missions but to pass on administrative legacies that tie us up in maintenance activity. I don't mean to imply that this is intentional. This often happens by default when local churches simply adopt past and outdated systems without critically examining the current worth and modern-day application of the system, or without determining whether their network of committees, teams, processes and protocols helps them stay focused on their purpose, mission and goals.

Whether we are planting new churches or leading existing churches, we have to do the hard work of re-visioning our systems to give people the freedom to focus on the mission side of the goal and not the maintenance side of the goal.

Mapping out our structure was one of the most difficult and time-consuming aspects of planting Impact Church. We researched other organizational models in church, academic, community and organizational structures. Each of these models was identified and studied to develop Impact's organizational system, a system that honors our denomination while keeping us focused on our mission and pushing the envelope into the future of church growth and organization.

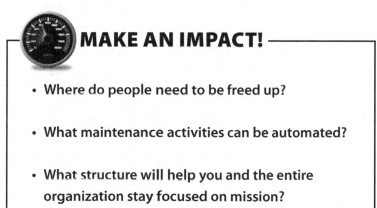

MAKE AN IMPACT!

- **Where do people need to be freed up?**

- **What maintenance activities can be automated?**

- **What structure will help you and the entire organization stay focused on mission?**

Impact Idea 78

Encourage Generative Ministry

Olu

In *Revolution in Leadership: Training Apostles for Tomorrow's Church*, Reggie McNeal inspires and reminds us that the local church must have a "proactive ministry agenda targeting people and their life issues and concerns."[17]

Organizational-thought guru, Peter Senge, illustrates this need in his account of adaptive organizations vs. learning organizations. Adaptive organizations are those organizations that fail to think ahead and simply duplicate what they are doing (and have always done) until something in their environment forces them to adapt. Learning organizations are those organizations that think ahead; those that develop products and resources that the customer will need in the future. Apple is an example of a learning organization. The company releases updates of new and improved products even as their sales are increasing in the older version. Recently, Apple outpaced the longtime IT leader, Microsoft.

If a new or existing church is to remain viable, it has to do the difficult work of thinking ahead and producing systems that make sense for today's customers (members) as well as potential customers (members) and future audiences. For some of you reading this book, that may mean thinking ahead of your denominational structure and doctrine.

In forming our leadership team, we looked at the denominational requirements and what we thought would be an organic approach that would enable us to sustain a rapid growth rate. We took a smaller leadership team approach and focused them exclusively on policy and governance. Our Lead Team operates at a high, vision-support level while staff and key volunteers manage the day-to-day ministry. The Leadership Team is comprised of people from the operational side of the house (personnel, trustees, finance and nominations) as well as our eight- member executive team. All have an equal voice and vote.

The notion of staff having voice and vote runs counter to many non-profit and faith-based board practices. It is common practice for staff to have voice, but no vote. We decided to buck this trend because it simply didn't make sense to have staff and key volunteers doing all the work and the board making all the decisions. When we come together to make decisions we recognized the need to have an equal part in determining the direction of the organization; to ensure that those who were fighting the war had a say in the next battle plans being designed by the Pentagon.

As a result of this clear division of labor and joint decision-making, those who are living the implementation of ministry on a daily basis are unencumbered by the armchair quarter-backing so often attempted by leadership boards/committees/councils. We also feel it is important that the "on the ground" perspective and the "removed" perspective are brought together in one place where strategic decisions that impact the future of the organization are made.

MAKE AN IMPACT!

How does your structure help you create a generative organization? Identify anything about your structure (including roles, responsibilities and decision-making processes) that leads your organization to being more generative than adaptive.

A "Learning Organization" is an organization that is continually expanding its capacity to create its future. For such an organization, it is not enough merely to survive. "Survival learning" or what is more often termed "adaptive learning" is important, indeed it is necessary.

But for a learning organization, "adaptive learning" must be joined by "generative learning," learning that enhances our capacity to create.[18]

~ Peter Senge

Impact 2010 High Level Structure View

Leaders
- Innovation
- Influence
- Coaching
- Execution

Vision

Leadership Team
- Governance
- Policy
- Wisdom
- Guidance

Impactors
- Ownership
- Ministry

Impactors (members), Leaders (staff and volunteers) and Leadership Team (both lay and staff) are all responsible for growing spiritually, leading, and visioning. Yet each has unique roles to play in the functioning of the overall organization.

Explore the "It" Factor

Olu and Edwin

Every time we talk to people about Impact, one of the first comments we hear is, "Man, the people got it at Impact." The minute you walk in or the minute you have an experience with Impact, you feel it.

Edwin often asks people to articulate what they mean when they say that Impact's got it, so we can keep working on it. They have a difficult time explaining what it is because it is radical. It is something that they have never experienced before. We have come to believe that it is created by our radical hospitality approach to everything we do.

Craig Groeschel is the lead pastor of Life Church in Oklahoma — one of the most innovative and rapidly-growing ministries in America. He has dedicated an entire book to the subject, *It: How Churches and Leaders can Get It and Keep It*. Throughout the book he takes us through the "you know it when you see it" references and then moves into what he has come to believe contributes to it:

- vision
- divine focus
- enjoying it with others
- innovative minds
- willingness to fall short
- outwardly-focused hearts
- kingdom-mindedness.

His advice? "If you want your ministry to have it, you must have it. When it has filtered through your heart — the rare combination of passion, integrity, focus, faith, expectation, drive, hunger, and God's anointing — God tends to infuse your ministry with it. He blesses your work. People are changed. Leaders grow. Resources flow. The ministry seems to take on a life of its own."[19]

"Learn as though you would never be able to master it; hold it as though you would be in fear of losing it." ~ Confucius

 **MAKE AN IMPACT!**

Do you have *it*? Does your ministry? Consider steps you can take to grow, feed and hold onto *it*. Have you ever experienced *it*? If not, go to a place others say has *it* and allow your subconscious mind and spirit to understand what *it* feels like.

Impact Idea 80

Choose Your Ruts Carefully

Olu

There is a sign at a junction on an Alaskan highway that reads: "CHOOSE YOUR RUT CAREFULLY; YOU WILL BE IN IT FOR THE NEXT 50 MILES." Like our organizations, unpaved roads can become rut-filled when exposed to extreme conditions of freezing/thawing or excessive rain. And I'm not sure you'll find more extreme conditions than church planting and church growth!

At Impact, we seek to be in a state of constant thaw and change so that we don't create ruts for ourselves. As an organization matures, however, it is natural for patterns to settle in. Those patterns — which started out as great solutions — can become limitations if they are not intentionally examined and evaluated.

Ultimately, we are limited by our vision for the future. There is nothing worse than a church or organization with vision failure. At Impact, the deadly sin is lack of vision; so we do everything within our power to create a DNA of creative vision. We quickly learned, wherever there is creative vision, there is also constant change. I sometimes joke and say, "Impact morphs each quarter." As I reflect on the comment, I am often reminded of how true it really is.

Each quarter, one or two aspects of Impact change. There may be a systems change, an area change, a personnel change, a theological change or a response to a global event. I am learning to live in an environment of change because I realize every great organization changes over time. As you look to the future, I hope you do not see current reality as the only possibility and get stuck in a rut. I hope you look to the future and see vision and embrace constant change.

We share all these thoughts with you to encourage you and so that God might be glorified and God's kingdom grown in your context. To learn more about Impact Church:

- visit us online: www.impactdcd.org
- follow us on Twitter
- become a fan on Facebook
- become a part of our LinkedIn network
- visit us the next time you are in Atlanta.

Blessings to you and your ministry!

Executive Vision Summary as Submitted to the North Georgia Annual Conference in 2006

Impact Church
The Start of a New Faith Community
Executive Vision Summary
Olujimi Brown
North Georgia Annual Conference
United Methodist Church

Vision
A multi-cultural gathering of people who are committed to sharing the love of Christ with the world.

Core Values / DNA
- Prayer
- Community/Economic Development
- Compassion
- Honesty
- Service

Ministry Focus / Mission Field
The focus of the ministry will be mission–based as opposed to maintenance–based as the congregation seeks to live out a "proactive ministry agenda targeting people and their life issues and concerns."20 The specific ministry focus will be to empower people by helping them realize their God-given potential. The mission field is an urban area that has experienced transition and economic decline.

Need

Each year hundreds of new churches are added to a laundry list of spiritual "fill-up" stations throughout the country and the world that advertise God's grace and mercy. This leads some to wonder if the "church limit" has been reached, and if an additional new church would be a spiritual overload. I agree with this line of thinking. The world does not need an additional common or carbon copy church; but the world does need many more cutting edge and relevant new churches that are willing to reach the people of the world for Jesus Christ in new and creative ways.

Location

The target area for the new church is Southwest Atlanta (West End). This urban/inner city location is ideal because: 1) it is located less than five miles from downtown Atlanta; 2) it is near three major interstate corridors; 3) it is adjacent to a Marta Station that is the "fifth busiest station" in Atlanta; 4) it is in close proximity to several of the most prominent colleges/ universities in America; and 5) it is a solid community, hosting some of the newest economic development sites in Atlanta.

Target Area Statistical / Spiritual Data:

www.link2lead.com 12/27/05

Current Population: 33,292

Households with No Faith Involvement: 25%

Average Age: 34.8

Average Household Income: $38,121

African-American: 90.9%

Increasing Ethnic Groups: Hispanic/Latino; Asian; Native American/Other

Description of the New Faith Community
The new faith community will attract:

- Non-believers/pre-Christians who have had no prior connection to the Christian Church.
- Believers in Christ who once were, but are no longer committed to the Christian faith.
- Committed Christians with the intention of helping them strengthen their faith and commitment to Christ.
- People of various races and cultures who are seeking a spiritual home.
- College students who are away from home.
- Homeless individuals who have no residence.

What Makes this New Faith Community Relevant and "Cutting-Edge?"

Holistic Salvation
Holistic Salvation is a concept adapted by Rev. Kirbyjon Caldwell, Senior Pastor of Windsor Village UMC in Houston Texas. This concept compels congregations to see each person as a whole being with spiritual, physical, mental, social, and economic needs. Therefore, the new church will seek to offer "Holistic Salvation" to all.[21]

24 Hours / 7 Days a Week
The three — five year projection is to begin offering services, recreation, worship, and counseling 24 hours a day and seven days a week to accommodate changing lifestyles, and to reach a greater number of people.

Space and Facility Design

The new church will consist of multiple facilities across the Metro Atlanta area. The initial facility will be an existing multi-use property to maximize ministry space. A current model would be a business retail strip, factory-warehouse or school building.

Technology

The entire facility will be technologically driven, utilizing the most innovative telephone, internet, video-television display, audio and video recording, messaging systems, signage, and lighting technology available.

Customer Service/Hospitality

It will be the goal of the congregation, clergy, and lay staff to always place customer service and hospitality at the forefront of the church's mission and ministry.

Focus on Children, Youth and Seniors

The new church will strive to plan and sponsor events that will have a positive effect on children, youth, and seniors.

Accountability and Cell Groups

The cell group format will build a cohesive community of believers, evangelize and seek out new believers, and impart instruction and direction to a large number of members on a consistent basis.

Life and Family Coaching

Each day there is an increasing need for the Church to offer extensive counseling services. The new church will use the innovative concept of life and family coaching to help people reach their fullest potential.

Economic Development

The core vision of the congregation gives emphasis to developing communities and serving as a change agent. Empowering people and their communities changes the world into a better place. The congregation will initiate both for-profit and non-profit organizations to achieve its goal of redeveloping and reinvesting in hurting communities.

Moving to Two Worship Experiences: Launch Priorities 8.07

Production Team

- Finalize technology acquisition plan (Include video recording and production plan)
- Finalize Overflow / Cry Room Plan
- September – December Budget Request (2 experiences)
- Order approved equipment
- Team Organization chart
- Hire additional staff persons
- Team training and walkthrough

Music Team

- September – December Budget Request (2 experiences)
- Team Organization Chart
- Order approved equipment
- Team Rehearsals and walkthrough

Clergy Team

- September – December Budget Request (2 experiences)
- Produce two service launch Clergy expectations
- October and November clergy worship assignments
- Team training and walkthroughs

Creative-Service Programming Team

- September – December Budget Request (2 experiences)
- September – December Worship Theme Calendar
- Team Organization Chart
- Service format changes
- Establish pre-production and live production meeting times
- Managing dual experience responsibilities: volunteers, set-up, etc.

Technology and Communications Team

- September – December Budget Request (2 experiences)
- Team Organization Chart
- Order approved equipment
- Evaluate effectiveness of Constant Contact / Re-Launch: October 07
- Re-Launch website: October 07
- Team training and walkthrough
- Develop job description for Tech. / Comm. Team Lead
- Managing dual experience responsibilities: cd duplication, etc.

Graphics Team

- September – December Budget Request (2 experiences)
- Team Organization Chart
- Order approved equipment
- Managing dual experience responsibilities: volunteers, two sets of sermon points, etc.
- Develop job description for Graphics Team Lead
- Team training and walkthrough

Children's Director
- Hire children's director
- Develop children's team

Finance Team
- September – December Budget Request (2 experiences)
- Order approved equipment
- Team organization Chart
- Managing dual experience responsibilities: volunteers, counters, security, check signers, etc.
- Continue working with Concierge team to develop most efficient method of operation
- Research process of obtaining bonded finance officials: signers, counters, etc.
- Team training and walkthrough

Hospitality Team
- September – December Budget Request (2 experiences)
- Order approved equipment: Offering envelopes, Envelope/ Card/Pen seat holders, etc.
- Team organization chart
- Develop additional creative hospitality ideas for worshipping guest: cookies, hot coco, etc.
- Lead plan in re-designing more welcoming/vibrant entry and exit points for worship center
- Managing dual experience responsibilities: volunteers, etc.
- Team training and walkthrough

Connection Groups: Impact small groups

- September – December Budget Request (2 experiences)
- Order approved equipment
- Team organization chart
- Develop additional creative ways to advertise who, what, when, and where.
- Finalize September – December plans
- Utilizing connection group members weekly to off er additional volunteers

Marketing Team

- September – December Budget Request
- Finalize marketing plans for launch
- Finalize implementation strategy (Short/Long-Term)

Facilities Team

- September – December Budget Request (2 experiences)
- Order approved equipment
- Team organization chart
- Managing dual experience responsibilities: volunteers, internal traffic flow, emergency evacuation, clean-up (between services), set-up, etc.
- Order more storage space: additional pod
- Develop plan to maintain order and cleanliness in storage spaces

Team training and walkthrough Host Team

- September – December Budget Request (2 experiences)
- Order approved equipment
- Team organization chart
- Managing dual experience responsibilities: volunteers, external traffic flow, etc.
- Team training and walkthrough

2nd Touch Team (visitor follow up and congregational care)

- September – December Budget Request (2 experiences)
- Order approved equipment
- Team organization chart
- Begin new movers contact system
- Develop additional creative ways to remain in contact with visitors, guests, etc:
- Send notes to individuals who are ill, bereaved, or celebrating births and birthdays.
- Team training

Servant Leaders Team

- September – December Budget Request (2 experiences)
- Order approved equipment
- Team organization chart
- Aggressively staff two experiences with volunteers
- Develop and implement Sunday meal plan
- Team training

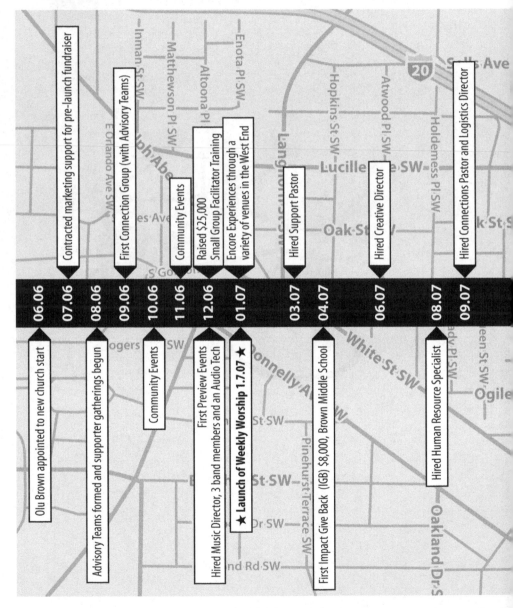

Contracted marketing support for pre-launch fundraiser

First Connection Group (with Advisory Teams)

Community Events

Raised $25,000
Small Group Facilitator Training
Encore Experiences through a variety of venues in the West End

Hired Support Pastor

Hired Creative Director

Hired Connections Pastor and Logistics Director

| 06.06 | 07.06 | 08.06 | 09.06 | 10.06 | 11.06 | 12.06 | 01.07 | 03.07 | 04.07 | 06.07 | 08.07 | 09.07 |

Olu Brown appointed to new church start

Advisory Teams formed and supporter gatherings begun

Community Events

First Preview Events
Hired Music Director, 3 band members and an Audio Tech

★ Launch of Weekly Worship 1.7.07 ★

First Impact Give Back (IGB) $8,000, Brown Middle School

Hired Human Resource Specialist

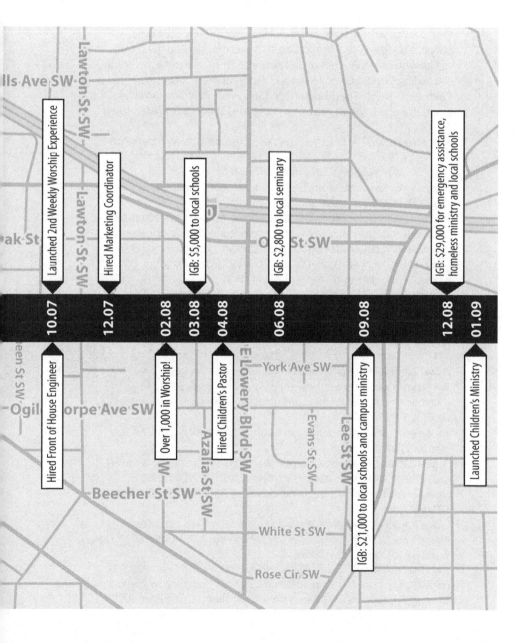

Launched 2nd Weekly Worship Experience

Hired Marketing Coordinator

IGB: $5,000 to local schools

IGB: $2,800 to local seminary

IGB: $29,000 for emergency assistance, homeless ministry and local schools

10.07

12.07

02.08

03.08

04.08

06.08

09.08

12.08

01.09

Hired Front of House Engineer

Over 1,000 in Worship!

Hired Children's Pastor

IGB: $21,000 to local schools and campus ministry

Launched Children's Ministry

End Notes

1 John Maxwell, *Thinking for a Change* (New York: Grand Central, 2003), 105–106.
2 Peter 2:9 But you are a chosen people, a royal priesthood, a holy nation, a people belonging to God, that you may declare the praises of him who called you out of darkness into his wonderful light. (NIV)
3 Jim Collins, *Good to Great* (New York: Harper Business, 2001) 44.
4 Caldwell, Kirbyjon, *The Gospel of Good Success: A Roadmap to Spiritual, Emotional and Financial Holeness* (New York: Simon & Schuster, 1999) 11–12.
5 Marty Neumeier, *The Brand Gap* (Berkeley, California: New Riders Publishing) 87–89.
6 http://www.trendsspotting.com/blog/?p=165
7 http://www.daviddalka.com/createvalue/2006/12/04/ses- chicago2006-day-1-advertising-in-social-media/
8 http://mashable.com/2009/04/08/facebook- from-100-to-200-million-users-in-8-months/http://www.apple.com/itunes/billion-app-countdown/?aosid=p204&siteid=1503186&program_id=2554&cid=OAS-EMEA-AFF&tduid=46a0c651061ca320b59220238e07f9eb
9 www.facebook.com/press/info.php?statistics
10 S. Truett Cathy, *It's Easier to Succeed Than to Fail* (Nashville, TN: Thomas Nelson Inc., 1989) 157.
11 Joe Gibbs, *Racing to Win* (Sisters, OR: Multnomah Publishers, 2002) 168.
12 John Maxwell, *Thinking for a Change* (New York: Warner Books, 2003) 114.
13 www.planningcenteronline.com
14 Jim Collins, *Good to Great* (New York: Harper Business, 2001) 44.
15 John Edmund Kaiser, *Winning on Purpose*. (Nashville: Abingdon Press, 2006) 125–127.
16 Bill Hybels, *Courageous Leadership* (Grand Rapids, Michigan: Zondervan, 2002) 81.
17 Reggie McNeal, *Revolution in Leadership: Training Apostles for Tomorrow's Church*. (Nashville: Abingdon Press, 1998) 24–26.
18 Peter Senge, The Fifth Discipline (Doubleday Business; 1st edition, 1994) 14.
19 Craig Groeschel, *It: How Churches and Leaders Can Get It and Keep It* (Grand Rapids, Michigan: Zondervan Publishing, 2008), Chapter 11: Do You Have It, Does It Have You?
20 John Maxwell, *Thinking for a Change* (New York: Grand Central, 2003).
21 Caldwell, Kirbyjon, *The Gospel of Good Success: A Roadmap to Spiritual, Emotional and Financial Holeness* (New York: Simon & Schuster, 1999)

CPSIA information can be obtained at www.ICGtesting.com
Printed in the USA
LVOW04s0759150415

434671LV00003B/5/P